THE
NEGOTIATION
FIELDBOOK

THE
NEGOTIATION
FIELDBOOK

Simple Strategies to Help
You Negotiate Everything

REVISED AND EXPANDED SECOND EDITION

GRANDE LUM

New York   Chicago   San Francisco   Lisbon   London
Madrid   Mexico City   Milan   New Delhi
San Juan   Seoul   Singapore   Sydney   Toronto

1 2 3 4 5 6 7 8 9 10   DOC/DOC   1 9 8 7 6 5 4 3 2 1 0

ISBN 978-0-07-174347-1
MHID 0-07-174347-2

This publication is designed to provide accurate and authoritative information in regard to the subject matter covered. It is sold with the understanding that neither the author nor the publisher is engaged in rendering legal, accounting, securities trading, or other professional services. If legal advice or other expert assistance is required, the services of a competent professional person should be sought.

—From a Declaration of Principles Jointly Adopted by a Committee
of the American Bar Association and a Committee of Publishers and Associations

McGraw-Hill books are available at special quantity discounts to use as premiums and sales promotions or for use in corporate training programs. To contact a representative, please e-mail us at bulksales@mcgraw-hill.com.

This book is printed on acid-free paper.

To my parents, Hampson and Evangeline Lum,
who nurtured and challenged me to do the best
I could and to give back whenever I could.

Contents

Foreword

Twenty years ago, two students and I wrote *Getting to Yes*, a primer on interest-based negotiation. Unlike prior books on negotiation that suggested bluffing, offering less than you expected to pay, demanding more than you expected to get, competing as to who could be more stubborn in making concessions, or demonstrating a greater willingness to walk away without agreement, our book was addressed simultaneously to negotiators on both sides. What was the best advice for one negotiator that was also the best advice for someone on the other side? That book has done well.

Yet little can be as satisfying to a teacher as to have a former student and colleague start with what he has been taught and go on from there. Grande goes far beyond whatever he learned from me. He has been consulting, training, and learning. He has tried out his ideas with dozens of organizations and companies.

And he has learned a lot about how people learn. Readers like to self-test to make sure they understand what they are reading. Learners like concepts formed in a way that makes them easy to remember. And everyone likes anecdotes and real-world examples.

Some years ago, when I asked one of my best students what she had learned in our negotiation workshop, she replied, "Three things: Prepare. Prepare. And prepare." Yes, and a reader of this fieldbook will also learn how to prepare and a great deal more. Another big lesson that comes through loud and clear is to appreciate the power of a collaborative approach.

We negotiate every day—in school, in business, in politics, in everything we do. Every time I want to influence someone or I deal with someone who wants to influence me, I am negotiating. For that world, this is perhaps the most useful book you will ever find.

Roger Fisher
Cambridge, Massachusetts

Preface

Since first writing *The Negotiation Fieldbook*, the book has been truly field tested. Businesspeople, lawyers, educators, students, and non-profit professionals from all over the world have read and implemented the ideas in the book. For the second edition, I have done my best to utilize the feedback I have received. The first edition was meant to put into operation a collaborative negotiation approach. In writing a second edition, that is still the ultimate goal, so I streamlined the concepts and added new topics critical to making a win-win approach more possible.

I particularly tried to focus on simplifying the advice for conducting negotiations. This meant making the second half of the book, particularly the chapters on the 4D approach more of a direct four-step approach. The four steps are (1) design, (2) dig for interests, (3) develop the options, and (4) decide. I also add more information on styles, agents, teaming, ethics, leverage, and offers in negotiation. Being a collaborative negotiator means being so when you are using your style, someone represents you, working in a team, making offers, and acting in an ethical manner. New to the second edition are Smart Negotiator Tips, which provide research-proven ways of operating more rationally.

Since writing the first edition, I became a clinical professor and director of the Center for Negotiation and Dispute Resolution at Hastings College of the Law. The second edition has been greatly influenced by my time in this vibrant program. Therefore, I would first like to thank my Hastings law students. These bright and curious people have taught me more than they will ever realize, and they renewed my passion for dispute resolution. Also I want to convey deepest thanks to my Hastings colleagues Melissa Nelken, Clark Freshman, Shauna Marshall, Jolynn Jones, Darshan Brach, Carol Izumi, and Chris Knowlton. Others who provided invaluable support were Heather Meeker-Green, Eric Collins, Irving Leung, David Mineta, Maya Pri-Tal, and Jane Palmieri. Last, I want to thank John Aherne of McGraw-Hill who approached me about doing this second edition. John was both a professional and a pleasure to work with.

I continue to be eternally grateful to those who helped make the first edition a reality. This includes Roger Fisher, Bruce Patton, Irma Tyler-Wood, Anthony Wanis-St. John, Glenn Hampson, Richard Morse, Monica Christie, Nan Santiago, Gianna Lum, and Garren Lum.

What was most gratifying about writing the first edition was that people who read it let me know what a difference it made in their careers and lives. To the extent that this second edition can continue to accomplish that, I will be greatly satisfied.

Introduction

In Tel Aviv, a Palestinian and an Israeli college student are trying to establish a dialogue for peace in the region. In Durham, North Carolina, the CEO of a biotech company is weighing a buyout offer. An auto union in Detroit is voting whether to go on strike. Two parents in Mexico City are discussing where to send their child to school.

What do these people have in common? In each case, they are confronting issues that require careful deliberation. They will try to negotiate their way to a solution, a new relationship, and a new understanding of each others' needs. Together, they will try to create new ways of working together that satisfy their concerns without resorting to haggling or manipulation.

Whether your challenge is resolving conflict or planning budgets, you negotiate your solutions. And the value of the outcome is not a matter of luck or coincidence. You expand the pie or create more value by negotiating wisely with the other parties.

But life does not automatically equip us to negotiate well. I have spent many years working with clients from every walk of life, including corporate executives, community leaders, politicians, teachers, diplomats, union presidents, clergy members, and lawyers. My goal is to help organizations and individuals improve the way they negotiate. What I find is that while negotiation is a necessary skill, it is not necessarily practiced.

In my work, people often come to me once they have reached an impasse. Clients are smart, capable human beings. But when there is a lot at stake and emotions are involved, negotiators can find themselves in situations they cannot dig their way out of. The negotiation elements I focus on in this guide have been used in these situations and in countless others when a solution seemed difficult or even impossible to achieve.

WHAT IS NEGOTIATION?

There are the obvious examples of negotiation—formal situations like diplomats creating peace treaties in the Middle East, union and management representatives working on a three-year contract, or two corporate teams figuring out the terms of a business-to-business partnership. Yet negotiating also happens at much more informal levels as well: a teenager arguing with a sister over using the family computer, or coworkers at a company determining responsibilities for a new project.

What are the common threads tying these experiences together? In this guide, as in my professional work, I define negotiation as any discussion to reach an agreement—which encompasses most any situation where people are trying to persuade and influence each other. So negotiation happens everywhere and in every setting.

I also define negotiating as a "cross-cultural" activity. Think of it this way: There can be a multitude of differences between two or more individuals who are negotiating—not just personality differences, but differences in experience, organizational backgrounds, family backgrounds, and more. These overlap with our individual qualities, making the way we communicate and manage conflicts rich and complex—cross-cultural.

My approach in this guide emphasizes the need to see things from the other person's perspective, to work in a joint fashion, and to create agreements that truly satisfy the critical interests of everyone involved.

THE PRIMARY GOAL OF THIS GUIDE IS TO TEACH YOU WHAT TO SAY AND DO IN ANY NEGOTIATION

There are many excellent books on negotiation. What has been missing until now is a book that focuses on conducting collaborative negotiations— specifically, a book that describes what to say in negotiation. Much of the advice found in the better negotiation books sounds good: "probe for interests beneath positions" or "use criteria to persuade," for example. The hard part is, of course, actually doing it. That's the need I address here—I give you the tasks and pieces of dialogue you need in order to improve.

This guide answers the following questions: How should you structure a negotiation and what should you do? What is the best way to begin a negotiation? What are the essential things you need to focus on to be successful? How do you sequence your moves? What do you do first and last? This guide gives you practical advice and introduces tools and exercises you can use to improve your negotiating.

Improving your ability to negotiate is easier than improving many other skills in life. Why? Because you negotiate all the time. At work or at home, many of your everyday interactions involve trying to influence and persuade others. Let's compare this to taking up a sport. If you took up golf, you would have to carve out time to go to the driving range or the golf course. A golf instructor once told me that 50 percent of the people he had taught over his lifetime never actually made it onto the golf course. Since negotiation happens all the time, your opportunities to improve never cease. This guide provides the tools to leverage those opportunities.

RECOMMENDING A PRACTICAL "EXPAND THE PIE" APPROACH

All parties in a negotiation should benefit from it and walk away as satisfied as possible. Many negotiations, after all, come down to unsatisfactory compromises that leave no one happy in the end. There are even times when walking away from a negotiation will be the best strategy or best outcome for you.

I recommend that you "expand the pie" as much as possible. Place a high value on helping your counterparts satisfy their interests and in building positive working relationships. The reality is that you cannot always get what you want. Unfortunately, people often approach their negotiations as if anything gained by one party must be taken away from another party. These people miss the chance to create value because they jump right to the "getting what's mine." How you negotiate determines the value you create. Expanding the pie (creating value) and cutting the pie (figuring out who gets what) are both critical tasks, and I provide my best advice on both.

By stressing what you should say, this guide is focused on improving communication and your working relationship with the other party as you negotiate. Parties in a negotiation are often stressed and find it difficult to communicate. By focusing on conducting the negotiation, I seek to provide some best practices on engaging the other person, asking helpful questions, putting the other person at ease, and making the process a truly collaborative one.

SMART NEGOTIATOR TIP

Don't Assume a Fixed Pie

People often go into tough situations and assume that if one side wins, the other side loses or more for you is less for me. Viewing things this way restricts the chance of collaboration or creating more value for both sides. The focus becomes beating the other side, and the parties are unable to see that the pie might be expanded.

Psychologist Leigh Thompson found that even when two negotiators want the same outcome, they accept a different settlement because they assume they must give up something to arrive at an agreement. Thompson called this an incompatibility bias, where a party assumes that his or her interests are incompatible with those of the other side. Thompson used a simulation in which negotiators should arrive at the same preference for two of the eight issues. However, 39 percent of negotiators failed to arrive at the optimal solution on at least one of the two issues. Interestingly, even when the parties do arrive at the seemingly collaborative agreement, neither side realizes that the other party has benefited as well.

Clearly many negotiations involve both sides wanting the same thing, and more for one side is less for the other. Do not let that fact crowd out creative opportunities. When you negotiate, consider the possibility that what you need may be compatible with what the other party needs.

THE METHOD PRESENTED IN THIS GUIDE WILL WORK WHETHER OR NOT THE OTHER SIDE PLAYS NICE

Clients constantly ask me if this method will work with individuals who are adversarial, positional, or difficult in some fashion. I write every page with the default assumption that the person across the table might be difficult and may not go along with an interest-based approach to negotiation. Everything I recommend is meant to improve your probability of success. This doesn't mean that you should approach every negotiation the same way. Whatever you do needs to fit your own personality and take into account the other person's style and the context in which you are having the discussion. In each chapter, I share how to adjust your approach for difficult situations. I also come back to the manipulative tactics that some people use (and some trainers teach!) and get you responding strategically to those tactics.

Asked and Answered

Difficult Tactics

Some people resort to "difficult" tactics to coerce the other party in a negotiation. It's how a lot of us were "taught" to conduct a negotiation—the stereotype of haggling with the used-car dealer. As you read on, you will learn that this isn't the best way to conduct business—that adding value to your negotiation is more likely to produce a win-win outcome. Some of the more popular tactics (and how you should respond to them) are described in Part Three of this guide.

Overview: The Negotiation Fieldbook

Key Concepts

The key concepts I lay out in this guide are how to:

- Have a clear plan for any negotiation
- Be fully prepared for any negotiation by having a clear understanding of goals, parameters, and strategy
- Be proactive in expanding and cutting the pie
- Be ready to deal with tactics that may arise.

If you read between the bullet points, you can see that all of these concepts have one bridging concept in common: Be prepared. Ten years from now, if you can recall only one concept from this guide, make it this one!

INDIVIDUALS AND ORGANIZATIONS NEED A SIMPLE, CONCISE NEGOTIATION BLUEPRINT

My ultimate goal with this fieldbook is to provide a solution for organizations and individuals who want to improve their negotiation skills on their own. You don't need a thousand unrelated tactics or complex academic theory. You need a simple, easy-to-follow blueprint that makes clear what effective negotiators actually say and do. Over the last 19 years I have experimented and learned innovative approaches to consulting, teaching, and coaching negotiation. Here I distill the best practices into one brief and concise resource manual. This guide will get you on your way to becoming a great negotiator!

Using *The Negotiation Fieldbook*

Readers familiar with *Getting to Yes* will recognize my emphasis on identifying the "elements" of negotiation. I identify these elements to help you understand what's happening when you negotiate. But understanding is only a first step. Focusing on these elements helps you and your team prepare for and conduct negotiations, expand the value in your negotiation, and get back on track if you reach an impasse.

As I discuss these elements of negotiation, I also provide advice on what to say and how to say it. Why is this important? In a conflict situation, negotiators try to see the conflict—rather than the people at the table—as the problem. This sounds sensible, yet it is often very difficult to do in reality. Therefore, in this guide I treat the dynamics and the outcome of a negotiation as inseparable. You are, after all, creating a working relationship as you negotiate. The *quality* of that working relationship will affect what happens at the table—*how you negotiate* will affect both the outcome and the relationship.

HOW CAN YOU MAKE THE MOST OF THIS FIELDBOOK?

Part One of this guide introduces the basic elements of negotiation—the substance of what you negotiate. These are Interests, Criteria, Options, and No-Agreement Alternatives, or "ICON." Part One of *The Negotiation Fieldbook* shows how success in any negotiation requires preparation in these four substance elements. It provides preparation forms on these four elements that will enable you to quickly prepare for any negotiation. The ICON elements can be briefly defined as follows:

Interests are the subjective needs, concerns, and desires of the parties. They are the basis from which people negotiate.

Criteria are objective benchmarks, precedents, and standards of legitimacy to filter and judge which options are best. Savvy negotiators come to the table with a good understanding of relevant benchmarks even before anything is agreed to.

Options are the possible solutions to which the parties might agree for satisfying their shared, differing, and conflicting interests.

No-Agreement Alternatives are what the parties will do if they walk away from the negotiation without coming to any agreement.

THE ICON NEGOTIATION MODEL

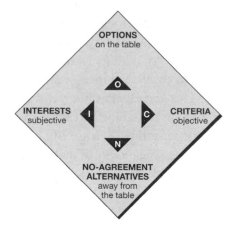

Part Two of this guide puts theory into practice by providing a step-by-step approach to negotiating from beginning to end. While ICON covers the substance elements of any negotiation, at least half of the battle is about how you get there, or conducting the negotiation. Therefore, the chapters in this second section describe how to communicate effectively and build working relationships as you negotiate. You accomplish this by using the "4D" approach:

STEP 1: You begin by **Designing** what the parties ⟨
negotiation for success. Your ability to be success⟩⟨⟩⟨⟩ ⟨⟩⟨ ⟨⟩⟨⟩
depends on what you do in the beginning by framing the negotiation, building rapport, setting goals, and having a clear plan.

STEP 2: You then move into **Digging** for interests by planning a
well-defined information exchange strategy. You can then share
and learn important background information and ask powerful
questions to understand each other's needs.

STEP 3: You follow up by **Developing** options to solve the problem at hand. By linking the underlying concerns, standards,
and precedents to proposals, you can create mutually agreeable
solutions.

STEP 4: Finally, you go to **Deciding** where the parties come to
closure by making offers and counteroffers. You will able to
close negotiations by using techniques that will help you decide
wisely and efficiently whether to agree or walk away.

If ICON provides an overall map of your negotiation, think of the 4D
approach as the directions for a specific upcoming negotiation session.

Here's a quick illustration of the 4D approach, applied to a negotiation between Nan, the vice president of human resources at ABC
Company, and Garren, a promising business school graduate who has
been called in for his third and final interview with the company.

In the **Design** step, Garren thinks carefully about his goals for the
interview and even considers what the goals of the hiring manager might
be. With these in mind, he drafts a proposed agenda for their meeting and
e-mails it to Nan. Being quite busy, Nan looks over the e-mail but doesn't
send a reply. Still, she is grateful for Garren's initiative and is happy to
have an agenda to follow. As their interview starts, Garren runs over the
agenda and tells Nan that he really wants to sign a contract that is fair and
good for both ABC and him.

In the **Dig** step, Nan and Garren begin working through the issues
that Garren has sequenced. Garren begins with issues he believes will be
easy, such as vacation time, and works toward salary and benefits.

In the **Develop** step, they work through options for each, Garren shares his research on what companies similar to ABC are offering and uses these to benchmark Nan's offer.

In the **Decide** step, with the terms of a draft contract in hand, both Nan and Garren have a decision to make. Garren asks himself, "Is this job better than one that pays me more but for which I will have to move to a more expensive city?" Similarly Nan asks herself, "Is this contract one that will work for ABC, as compared with contracts I might offer similar candidates?"

Part Three of this guide looks at what to do before you get to the negotiating table. This section contains an important chapter on strategizing fully and looks at different negotiation styles, different types of negotiations, the mode of the negotiation, and more. This section also contains a list of difficult negotiation tactics and how to deal with them, as well as observations on preparation and dealing with negotiations as cross-cultural experiences.

Part Four, the Appendix, provides other resources including a glossary, references, and extra negotiation worksheets.

The different sections of this guide are arranged to give you a full overview of negotiating in what I think is a logical sequence. In practice, go through this guide in the order that makes the most sense for you, particularly if you are already an experienced negotiator. If you want to learn how to walk away in negotiation because that's what you're facing, then turn to that section first. If you want to learn how to deal with the Cherry-Picking tactic, go directly to it.

Negotiation is both reflective and active: clear thinking and decisive action are both required to improve your outcomes. This guide is designed so you can quiz yourself to determine whether you understand the concepts, write answers to help you internalize the difference between them, and analyze your own negotiations. It's important, therefore, to write in this guide! Why? Because while it may not be rocket science, putting negotiation concepts into play doesn't come easy—especially if it's a high-stakes, high-risk, or emotional negotiation. So practice here with me, and you'll be ready for any negotiation. The Appendix of this guide contains copies of all the negotiation worksheets. Choose which set you would rather fill out and keep the other set free for analyzing your other negotiations.

Let's start now by thinking ahead in order to set out your goals for this experience. Imagine you have finished working through this guide and are now a better negotiator. What are you doing differently? Use the worksheet provided below to answer this question.

Negotiation Worksheet

This guide will come alive if you have at least one challenging negotiation of your own in your head as you read. Think of one that's happening now or is about to happen (rather than one that's already done). Consider one where you could really benefit from reflection. Write your answers on the worksheet that appears below.

Throughout the rest of the guide I will provide places for you to write in information on this specific negotiation, which will provide a systematic and rigorous analysis of your situation.

Your Negotiation Worksheet

1. With whom are you negotiating? (person, position, experience, organization)

   _____

   _____

   _____

2. What are at least three key pieces of background information on this negotiation? List them.

   _____

   _____

   _____

3. Why is this negotiation a challenging one for you?

   _____

   _____

   _____

   _____

THE
NEGOTIATION
FIELDBOOK

PART ONE

THE ICON NEGOTIATION MODEL

Negotiation can be absolutely frustrating when you don't have a road map for the terrain ahead. You may be about to negotiate something that will impact your organization, career, family, or finances, but you may have no idea how to approach the interaction, let alone how to prepare for it systematically.

[ICON Value Diamond graphic: OPTIONS on the table (top), INTERESTS subjective (left), CRITERIA objective (right), NO-AGREEMENT ALTERNATIVES away from the table (bottom)]

The first section of this guide presents the building blocks of negotiation. These four interlocking elements of Interests, Criteria, Options, and No-Agreement Alternatives will help you through the chaos of negotiation by providing four categories of information that enable you to be fully organized and prepared.

I call the graphic on this page the ICON Value Diamond because each element is a source for creating more value.

Interests: Get Underneath Negotiating Positions

Interests *underlie positions. They are subjective—the needs, goals, drivers, concerns, and fears of each party.*

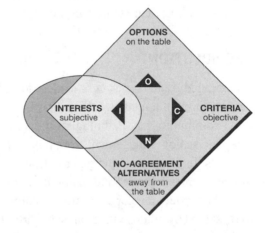

THE CHALLENGE

In the late 1980s and early 1990s, the health-care system of a major U.S. metropolitan area was widely acclaimed for being able to provide effective coverage and care for local residents at a low cost. Cooperation among the area's hospital systems, insurance providers, governments, and businesses received nationwide praise. The situation worsened over the next several years, however, resulting from changes in the health-care environment, government deregulation, and leadership turnover at the hospital systems. By the late 1990s, one of the area's largest hospitals was forced to shut its doors, physicians shuttled from one system to another lured by politicking and benefits, and the business community watched as health-care costs increased relentlessly.

In 2001, the local business community sought to change this dynamic and reduce health-care costs. A major health insurer forced the matter by issuing an RFP (request for proposals) for medical laboratory testing, with the goal of lowering its reimbursement costs for these services. After local hospital systems were unable to develop a collaborative agreement, two submitted a joint bid, and the third joined with a fourth hospital to submit a competing bid. A cycle of exclusion and collusion developed, forcing a race to the bottom in which even the winning bidders would regret their bids. Because of a lack of trust, the hospitals found it easier to disrupt each other's bidding than create a community-based, collaborative solution.

THE SOLUTION

Encouraged by local business leaders to return to the bargaining table, the parties, through a mediator, began probing each other's interests in designing a community lab. Pathologists, lab operations managers, financial officers, and senior management from hospital systems shared their underlying interests. Interests that emerged as critical were reducing duplication, creating economies of scale, and maintaining or improving the quality of care.

The group developed a solution calling for the creation of a new entity to be shared by all hospital groups: a "virtual" lab that would channel testing according to agreed-upon guidelines and that had a single reimbursement rate (between this new entity and the insurance companies). As negotiations progressed, however, the parties still lacked a common ground on the business and operational vision of their new venture. In particular, the parties found it difficult to discuss reimbursement without feeling threatened. Outside commercial lab administrators serving similar markets helped unify their objectives. By the end of the negotiation, the hospitals had designed a reimbursement plan to be negotiated with insurers. The reimbursement rate issue was the critical final hurdle to reaching an agreement.

Two days before the deadline, all parties signed the framework agreement to create the new community medical testing lab and agreed with insurers on a reimbursement rate that saved the community millions of dollars annually. The proposed new lab also incorporated a new information system to provide unprecedented secure access to patient lab results for all area physicians, especially for patients whose records were associated with more than one hospital.

Interests are the nuts and bolts of agreements. They are the concerns, drivers, incentives, underlying needs, and motivators of the parties. They are the reasons people are involved in a negotiation in the first place. Interests have been the focus of some of the best research and writing on negotiation, including the work of Roger Fisher, William Ury, David Lax, and James Sebenius.

Interests are not the same as positions. For negotiation purposes, I define positions as the demands of the parties. Another way of explaining the difference between interests and positions is to say that positions are what you *want*, while interests are what you *need*.

People sometimes make the simple mistake of negotiating on the basis of stated or implied demands. Understanding that important interests underlie demands is a powerful insight into negotiation because you free yourself from having to respond to and counter with demands of your own, which are often extreme and unreasonable.

Overview: INTERESTS

Focusing on Interests

- Uncovers the other person's concerns, drivers, incentives, underlying needs, and motivations
- Allows you to share your interests, so that they can be satisfied
- Lays the groundwork for creating a multitude of options
- Prevents you from getting stuck in useless conflicts and stalemates
- Sets the stage for making fair decisions based on legitimate criteria

Bottom Line

Interests are the foundation of successful negotiations.

For instance, consider this typical example of positional negotiating (see the flowchart below):

CUSTOMER: How much do you want for that black velvet picture of Elvis?

STOREKEEPER: This one, the one signed by the King himself? I suppose I could let it go for $500.

CUSTOMER: Whoa! That's out of my league. (Starts heading toward the door)

STOREKEEPER: Well, seeing that you're such an aficionado, I'll give you a special deal for $425.

CUSTOMER: Well, I am in a rush to get to the airport, so tell you what, I'll give you $175 for it.

STOREKEEPER: This is a one-of-a-kind collector's item. I've owned it for 10 years. I could never let it go for less than $350.

CUSTOMER: $200 is my final offer.

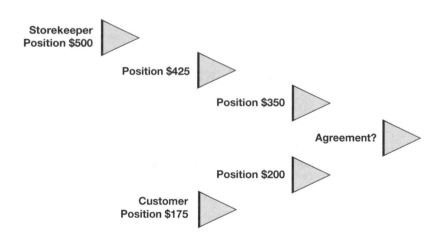

For the most part, these negotiators are focused on price and numbers. Sometimes this feels like the best path to a quick and satisfying conclusion to a deal. This is often the case for one-time, low-value transactions, such as buying items at a garage sale or a bazaar where haggling is the accepted "game." But what happens if you're negotiating over something of more value to you? Haggling is not the best strategy for life's more complex relationships. Even when you're buying a new car, price haggling alone never fully addresses your varied interests in price, financing, rebates, options, and so on. Positional bargaining becomes increasingly painful, costly, and inefficient as the complexity of the negotiation and importance of the deal increases.

Addressing interests is the first key to unlocking yourself from the trap of positional bargaining. Interests are the reasons underlying positions. While there is only one way to satisfy a position, there are *many* ways to satisfy an interest. And the more an agreement satisfies the parties' interests, the better the deal.

Imagine for a moment that Helen Hoops, a top women's professional basketball player, is renegotiating her contract with the San Francisco Golden Gaters. She has just ended an all-star season. Helen's agent, Monique Lee, and the team's general manager, Kerry West, will be discussing the potential deal.

PRINCIPAL PARTIES	NEGOTIATING AGENTS FOR THE PRINCIPAL PARTIES
Helen Hoops	Monique Lee, Helen's agent
Golden Gaters owner George Sunburger	Kerry West, Gaters general manager

Let's look at the interests of the two principals (see the table on the following page). If Monique (Helen's agent) and Kerry (the Golden Gaters general manager) truly understand each other's interests, they can craft an agreement that meets their underlying needs well. Monique and Kerry should also identify their high-priority interests. For Helen, these include getting the best possible deal and long-term security. The Golden Gaters' first priority is to create a foundation for continued success. Without understanding interests, the negotiators will likely resort to haggling over dollars and leave value on the table unclaimed by either party.

HELEN'S INTERESTS	TEAM OWNER'S INTERESTS
• Get the best deal possible	• Win the league championship
• Long-term security	• Create a foundation of continued success
• Show that she's still one of the best	• Spur ticket sales
• Be respected	• Attract other talented ballplayers
• Stay in the area where she grew up	• Stay within budget
• Win the championship	• Deal with cash-flow problems
• Retire as a Golden Gater	• Avoid setting unfavorable salary precedents
• Get more commercial endorsements	• Keep team morale high
• Be treated like a star	• Satisfy minority owners
• Increase accomplishments to match past stars	• Keep fans loyal, happy, and interested in the team
• Have opportunity to increase individual records	• Make sure Helen doesn't get injured
• Make money	
• Increase her value for her next profession	
• Leverage her value in related business activities	
• Be free to engage in hobbies	

Truly effective negotiators know the interests of the individuals across the table and other decision makers away from the table. This gives them insight into what kind of a deal they can craft and what type of offers they can make that will be valuable to all. Asking about these interests is a much more powerful approach than guessing. For one, making assumptions like, "They want to make more money," may not be valid—the true interest may be, "to start preparing for retirement." Demonstrating genuine desire in finding a mutually beneficial resolution to a problem will go further than simply pitting your interests against what you perceive to be theirs.

AGENT'S INTERESTS	GENERAL MANAGER'S INTERESTS
• Increase number of players represented	• Have the best possible team on the court
• Establish reputation as top agent	• Create the infrastructure for a successful team
• Get best possible deal for her client	• Keep the owner satisfied
• Build and keep excellent relationship with the team	• Increase ticket sales
• Earn a high commission	• Enhance team popularity
	• Attract top-quality players
	• Keep player salaries within limits
	• Increase value of marketing deals

Let's look at the interests of other parties who will have an impact on the deal between Helen and the team. For now, let's explore the interests of Monique Lee, the player's agent, and Kerry, the general manager (see the table above).

Once we examine the interests of all the parties with a stake in the outcome, including the player and the team, our perspective on the negotiation and our thoughts about possible solutions may evolve. This examination is vital intelligence for any negotiator, but is often over-looked because people tend to focus on positions. It is more challenging and rewarding to discover underlying interests because they are what motivated us to come to the negotiation table in the first place.

Interests are not necessarily fixed or written in stone. Yours may shift as you negotiate, which means that you need to be aware of your interests at all times. Indeed, how you perceive your own interests and how your interests are perceived by others is another overlooked but important aspect of negotiating. The least helpful perception for either party is that, "You will give in to my demands, or I will give in to yours."

In order to reach valuable agreements that everyone can live with, interests have to be met and satisfied. Positions are often little more than opening demands and should be treated as such.

Asked and Answered

Asking Questions

Asking questions to discover the other party's interests is the "Dig" step of the 4D approach discussed in Part Two of this guide. There are questions to ask that can help the process along—you won't need to blurt out something indelicate like, "What in the world are you thinking!"

If you look at the tables listing the interests of various parties in the Helen Hoops-Golden Gaters negotiation, you are likely to find several things an effective negotiator looks for: shared interests, differing interests, and interests that may actually be conflicting (for instance, salary compensation: Helen wants more and the Golden Gaters would prefer to pay less). Obviously, you can create attractive proposals, packages, and offers by knowing (or at least guessing) how all these interests relate to each other.

Examine the following table of interests to get a sense of some of the shared, differing, and conflicting interests in this negotiation between Helen and the owner. Shared interests are those the parties have in common. Differing interests are just that, different—not held in common, but also not at odds with the other party. Conflicting interests are not only differing, but they are in some fashion in tension with each other. For example, both Helen and George share an interest in having the team do well. Helen may be indifferent to the owner's concern about the sale value of the team—she may not have a strong opinion one way or the other. At first glance, their salary interests may conflict since more money for Helen means less for George.

As you can see, though, many interests are shared by Helen and the team. Although positions and demands might seem opposed when the agent and team management first meet, they share many underlying goals. Relatively few of their interests are actually in conflict. With those that are, a creative negotiator will look for even deeper layers of interests in order to find some point at which the interests complement each other.

INTERESTS	CONFLICTING	SHARED	DIFFERING
• Maximize salary for Helen	√		
• Increase possible sale value of team			√
• Improve team standing and performance		√	
• Maximize Helen's freedom to engage in hobbies (e.g., motorcycling)	√*		
• Attract top players to team		√	
• Increase ticket sales		√	
• Preserve team budget for salaries			√
• Maximize agent commission			√
• Obtain corporate/product endorsements for Helen		√	

*Team prefers lowest risk possible of Helen getting injured.

Indeed, you build negotiation value by *understanding* the parties' differing interests and the priorities they assign to them. Not all interests are created equal, after all, so understanding whether they are of high, medium, or low priority will help you reach agreements by making sure higher-priority interests are satisfied first. This is an important step—negotiation requires understanding as much as it does persuasion and influence.

Once priorities are assigned, both parties can begin understanding each other's motivations and begin working toward an agreement. The first step is to recognize the importance of assigning priorities and then look more deeply for differences, similarities, and conflicts. Examine the table at the top of the next page. Both parties are clearly interested in limiting tax liabilities this year, for instance; keeping down the up-front costs of the team is an area where both parties can find immediate agreement.

PRIORITY LEVEL	HELEN'S SALARY PRIORITIES	OWNER'S BUDGETARY PRIORITIES
High	• Retain freedom for endorsements • Limit tax liability this year	• Limit fixed-costs growth this year • Maximize confidentiality of salaries paid
Medium	• Retire at highest salary ever (in two years)	• Attract top talent • Defer new signing costs
Low	• Maximize cash now	• Minimize tax liabilities this year • Preserve budget flexibility for anticipated windfall next year

The following scenario offers you an opportunity to practice understanding interests.

SCENARIO

Darrin and Wayman are the co-owners of a restaurant. Darrin is also the restaurant's head chef. The two are trying to renegotiate the terms of their partnership. Their conversation has been heated. Here are some of their statements. Take a guess at their interests. Write your answers on the worksheets that follow.

WAYMAN'S STATEMENTS	WAYMAN'S POSSIBLE INTERESTS
• Hey, I invested $200,000, so I deserve what I get. • You've always insulted my taste in everything. • If it weren't for me, you wouldn't see this place half full. • I had no say in hiring the sous chef.	

DARRIN'S STATEMENTS	*DARRIN'S POSSIBLE INTERESTS*
• You have to give me 25 percent more of the profit. I'm here day and night.	
• I'm the one who started this restaurant.	
• I can't stand all your meddling with the kitchen. You almost started a fight with my sous chef during our busiest week.	

Right away we can see that Darrin and Wayman are both looking for more recognition from each other. This might be a good starting point for finding common ground.

A few possible answers are listed below—possible interests of these two parties.

DARRIN'S POSSIBLE INTERESTS
- Clearly he has financial interests, but he may be concerned about his investment of time and energy relative to return.
- Gaining recognition and acknowledgment
- Maintaining staff morale and a positive work environment

WAYMAN'S POSSIBLE INTERESTS
- Getting a good return on his investment
- Gaining recognition and acknowledgment
- Maintaining respect and politeness

SMART NEGOTIATOR TIP

Do the Tough Job of Putting Yourself into Their Shoes

Why is it hard? Because people tend to think they see the world as it is and if someone else sees it another way, they are naive, ignorant, or worse. People also tend to take credit for their own success and blame others when things go badly. They tend to believe information that supports their opinions and beliefs while disregarding information that challenges or contradicts their opinions and beliefs. All these things make it difficult to truly see the world from the other side's perspective. This is especially true if conflict and hostility smolders between the parties.

Social psychologist Lee Ross researched naive realism, a conviction that the person sees the world as it is, and when people do not see it similarly, they do not see the world as it is. People are generally very good at spotting bias in others, but not in themselves. Ross found that in the Israeli-Palestinian conflict, both Israelis and Palestinians who viewed the same media coverage of an event perceived bias. Israelis saw bias in favor of Palestinians, while Palestinians saw bias in favor of Israelis. Ordinary group discussion can polarize the view, because it shifts toward right and wrong. By having group members articulate one argument that the other side makes that holds legitimacy, 100 percent of the subjects were led to a potential solution for the conflict.

For you as a negotiator, ask the other party to share an interest or an argument that has merit. You are not asking that party to agree, but you are making it more possible to reach an agreement. You can also do the same by articulating one argument of the other party that has legitimacy.

SUMMARY

- Interests are the foundation of successful negotiation.
- Interests can be shared, differing, or conflicting.
- Understanding interests that underlie positions or demands frees you from having to respond or counter with positions or demands of your own.
- Prioritizing interests as you prepare to negotiate will help you reach agreement.

QuickGuide: Interests

Definition	Interests are the motivators, needs, drivers, concerns, and fears of the parties.
Importance	Interests are the foundation for the entire negotiation—the reasons for being in a negotiation.
Preparation	Understand your interests and spend some time contemplating the interests of the other side. Discover the priorities.
Dialogue	Question: "What are the underlying reasons for this proposal?" Statement: "What I really care about here is setting a precedent that works for the entire organization and others who follow you."
Tips	Put yourself in the other person's shoes to understand his or her interests. Focus on shared interests.

YOUR NEGOTIATION WORKSHEET

Now let's focus on your own negotiation—the one you jotted down earlier. Spend some time listing the interests of the various parties involved in the negotiation on the worksheet on the following page. Then indicate whether these interests are shared, differing, or conflicting, and also identify the priority level of the interests.

Your Negotiation Worksheet

Interests	Type	Priority
Yours		
Theirs		
Other Stakeholders		

Type	Priority
S=shared	H=high
D=differing	M=medium
C=conflicting	L=low

REVIEW (*SEE ANSWER KEY AT END OF CHAPTER*)

Check all that apply

1. What are interests?
    - __ a) The underlying needs, concerns, and motivations of the parties
    - __ b) Proposals for agreement
    - __ c) The foundation of effective negotiation
    - __ d) Objective standards, benchmarks, and precedents

2. What is a position?
    - __ a) A demand that a party makes at the outset of a negotiation
    - __ b) The fear a person expresses—his or her "driver"
    - __ c) A single solution that is presented as the right answer for agreement
    - __ d) A clue to a person's underlying interests

3. When comparing the interests of parties in a negotiation, look for those that are:
    - __ a) shared, difficult, and constant
    - __ b) shared, differing, and constant
    - __ c) shared, differing, and conflicting
    - __ d) bizarre, outrageous, and funny

Is the statement conveying an interest or a position?

1. We are *not* painting the house yellow.
2. We need to price this project at $15,500.
3. We will need to satisfy our safety concerns.
4. We *must* have five more community members on this project.
5. I am worried about the lack of resources that are allocated.

True or False

___1. Interests are unchanging indicators of what parties really want.

___2. Interests lie just below the surface demands parties make and are always just one layer down.

_____3. Parties can assign different values and priorities to their various interests.

_____4. Prioritizing interests is a waste of time because they change.

ANSWER KEY

Check all that apply

1. What are interests?
   a) Yes. This is the fundamental definition of interests.
   b) No. When someone makes a proposal, this is a position. The underlying needs behind the statement would be the interests behind that proposal.
   c) Yes. Understanding the interests of the parties is the key to successful negotiations.
   d) No. Interests are subjective rather than objective.

2. What is a position?
   a) Yes. This is the fundamental definition of a position.
   b) No. While fears and drivers may lead a party to state a position, they are still interests. Whether the other party views them as rational or not, fears are "subjectively" believed by the person holding them.
   c) Yes. A position is a solution that is presented as the "right" answer.
   d) Yes. By figuring out the "why" of the stated position, parties are uncovering the interests.

3. When comparing the interests of parties in a negotiation, look for those that are:
   c) shared, differing, and conflicting.

Is the statement conveying an interest or a position?

1. Position. There is no explanation as to what interests are being met by painting the house yellow.

2. Position. Even though the word "need" is used, there is a focus on one solution.
3. Interest. No specific demand is being made on *how* to go about meeting the interest in safety. The statement does convey assertiveness. Many options could potentially satisfy the interest.
4. Position. No explanation is given as to what interests are being served by the number of community members on the project.
5. Interest. No precise demand is given regarding how to go about meeting the interest in adequate resource.

True or False

1. False. Interests are often dynamic. They change as our perspectives and situations change. We *can* influence how others see their *own* interests.
2. False. Interests can be quite deep and multilayered. Parties may have more than one interest on any issue, and your interests may not always be in perfect harmony with each other.
3. True. Prioritizing is a key to enhancing negotiation.
4. False. Knowing the most important interests at a specific time makes it more likely that the parties can reach an agreement.

Criteria: Use Objective Standards

Criteria *are precedents, bench-marks, and standards. They serve as "objective" means to filter or narrow the options.*

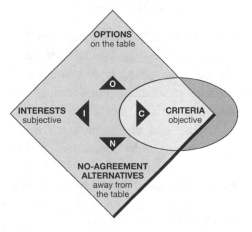

THE CHALLENGE

Gianna is a senior manager at the Paris office of GLNS, one of the largest consulting firms in the world. She has been attempting to transfer to the Manila office for the last six months because her husband has found a dream job there. Betty is the human resources (HR) officer responsible for Manila and has been demanding that Gianna sign a noncompetition clause stating that if Gianna leaves GLNS, she cannot join another consulting firm or create her own consulting company in Manila. Gianna is concerned that if her job at GLNS Manila does not work out, she might be stuck there, unable to make a living or practice her profession.

In the initial meeting between Gianna and Betty, Gianna expresses shock when she hears about the noncompetition clause. Never having come across such a clause in any of her professional experiences, Gianna is at a loss for words. Betty (who has a reputation for being hard-nosed) says to Gianna, "We have been burned in the past, which is why we inserted this clause." Gianna has been at GLNS for five years, has always had excellent reviews, and is in line for partnership. While she does not want to throw that away, she does not want to risk being in a situation where she cannot earn a living doing what she enjoys if things don't work out. She feels cornered.

THE SOLUTION

Gianna asks for another meeting with Betty and her new manager Soon-yu. Before the meeting, Gianna sends an e-mail to Betty and Soon-yu which states, "I am willing to do some research on noncompetition clauses. What information would you find useful?" Soon-yu replies that she wants to know what other offices do. Betty replies that she has this information in her files.

Gianna begins her research. She speaks to the HR person in the Paris office to get a better understanding of French and international HR contracts. She calls an HR lawyer in Manila and discusses the enforceability of such clauses. She asks other GLNS employees and finds out they do not have such a clause in their contracts. She also finds that three employees recently left to start a competing firm after spending less than one year at the Manila office. What management seemed most upset about was that these were international transfers. The firm invested in these employees, paying their relocation costs, securing visas, providing training, awarding bonuses, and conducting orientation, and then got shortchanged.

At their next meeting Gianna shares her research with Betty and Soon-yu. Soon-yu then asks about the standard global contract. Gianna replies, "I have a copy here. I'm sure you have a copy in your files. Correct me if I'm wrong, Betty, but the standard contract has no such noncompetition clause."

"Yes," agrees Betty. "However, HR has the leeway to add clauses to the contract at our discretion."

"I can understand that," Gianna says, "although I think their enforceability, particularly abroad, is debatable. I can send along some analysis done by a Manila lawyer if you'd like."

Betty and Soon-yu agree to look at the lawyer's information.

Gianna continues, "I'd like to know more about your desire for this clause."

"I don't want to go into the details," says Betty, "but suffice it to say that we are concerned about our people, particularly international transfers, going to the competition."

"That's understandable," replies Gianna. "Let's see if we can figure out something so all parties feel fairly treated. Betty, it sounds like you have a lot of information I don't have. I'd be curious to understand how other recent international transfers have been handled."

Soon-yu echoes Betty's earlier statement. "We are interested in protecting the firm for the future, and protecting our investment in moving employees abroad."

Gianna acknowledges the high cost of bringing someone like her to a foreign office. "Would a two-year employment contract resolve the impasse?" she asks. "The firm can be reassured I will stay in Manila for a defined time period."

Betty and Soon-yu acknowledge that this would ease their concerns, as well as ensure continuity and stability in the Manila office.

Gianna also states, "I don't see this as a minimum. I am committed to this firm. I think it's important to agree to a two-year clause if that will reassure you."

The three agree, and the noncompetition issue is dropped.

Overview: CRITERIA

Negotiating on the Basis of Criteria

- Ensures that no party feels "taken" by the deal
- Provides a rational, neutral approach to deciding among multiple options
- Gives negotiators the power of precedents and accepted standards
- Protects negotiators against manipulation

Bottom Line

Criteria are principles that help measure the fairness of a negotiated deal.

In many negotiations, simply discussing interests and options is sufficient to reach agreement because of how much the pie expands as you talk.
However, some negotiations cannot be resolved solely by creating options
that meet the parties' interests, especially if there is a financial or numerical
decision to be made and a division of value has to take place. Even when one
party wants to purchase an automobile and the other wants to sell it, the question of price still remains—the seller wants to get more, and the buyer wants
to give less. In cases like these, it is necessary to spend some time evaluating
with criteria to produce a solution that is fair to all parties at the table.

Criteria refer to the standards, external benchmarks, commonly
accepted procedures, and precedents we can point to as we negotiate. Think
of criteria as the objective part of a negotiation and interests as the subjective
part. Understanding criteria helps provide a landscape of possible options
and helps identify what range of solution you can assert. Use criteria to
determine what options are fair, to alter and narrow the options, and to move
toward a possible commitment or final agreement.

In more adversarial negotiations, criteria are deliberately ignored, for-
gotten, or set aside. Adversarial negotiators tend to exert their will, hoping
that, just by being stubborn, they will get their way. The winner of a willpower contest is the one who can hurt or intimidate the other more, or make
the other feel guiltier or just worn out and desperate. In contrast, those using
criteria tend to be more focused on reason, fairness, and rationality, and the
agreements they get yield greater satisfaction.

You often have an audience when you negotiate. Even if they are not
in the room, they are waiting for you to deliver results. Chances are that
you frequently need to report what happened in your negotiations to other
people to whom you have some accountability. These people might be
your boss, your shareholders, the members of the union you represent, your
spouse, your children, your management team, and/or anyone else who is
relying on you to negotiate well. What people sometimes find surprising is
that by using criteria to negotiate, they are in a powerful position to explain
the outcome of the negotiation to their audience. Which would you find
easier to say to your spouse: "They gave me fair market value for the used
car, rather than the trade-in value," or "Well, the dealer gave us $3,000 less
than we were hoping for our old car." The criteria do the explaining to some
extent.

Have you ever reached an agreement quickly with someone, only to have a vague sense of regret soon after? Some call this feeling the "winner's curse" (Bazerman and Neale in *Negotiating Rationally*). In haggling situations, the feeling may be justified because, indeed, you may have given in too quickly, but most of the time that feeling is based on the idea that you might have done better for yourself if only you had held out longer. Using criteria is one way to protect yourself against this sensation.

Let's return to Helen Hoops's contract negotiation to see how using criteria would apply to her situation. If we limit ourselves to the financial compensation issues for a moment, there are several precedents or benchmarks that help create a rational range for negotiation.

CRITERIA FOR HOOPS NEGOTIATION	VALUE
Helen's previous contract compensation	$1 million
What highest paid Gater Leslie Lisette earns	$800,000
What other stars like Regina Miller make	$2 million
What NY Turnkeys are offering Helen	$1.2 million
Total team budget for the open position	$4.5 million (set by owner)
Average contract value for basketball center	$500,000
What a superstar center would cost	$1.5 million
What TV/radio/advertising pays to Gaters	$1 million

Occasionally, negotiators can find no easily accessible precedents, criteria, or benchmarks they can point to for a fair outcome. Negotiators also run into problems when they get stuck on competing standards. In these cases, I recommend several possible moves. First, if you don't find any criteria, consider jointly creating some that will serve the parties well. For example, you might brainstorm new ways to measure a fair outcome if you and your spouse are deciding how much television your four-year-old son should be watching. Your spouse may not mind if Henry watches two hours of morning cartoons, especially if they are on the public television channel. However, you might have other concerns beyond the content of the programming: "Honey, the kids seem to be watching so much TV that they don't want to come to breakfast. This is making us late for school and work. Why don't we try—for one week only—a limit of two half-hour cartoons and see how that works? After the week is over, we can consider how well this worked."

When you have the opposite problem—too many criteria, some of which are in conflict with each other—then I recommend doing one of two things. The first is to negotiate over the preferred standards both parties have, and have each party explain how his or her preferred standard meets the interests of fairness of the other side. Another possibility is to look at the competing standards and create a new, overarching or hybrid standard.

For example, in international negotiations, most countries adhere to the principle that no country has the right to interfere in the internal affairs of another country—the domestic jurisdiction standard. At the same time, some international issues are important enough to warrant one country looking carefully at the internal actions of another. There are also international problems that cannot be contained within the borders of a single country—industrial air pollution, global warming, and depletion of the ozone layer, for instance. If negotiators are imaginative and creative enough, they may even establish a new standard or landmark to serve as a model for others.

The use of river water when the river runs through several countries has often been an international issue with a negotiated agreement. If each country simply did as it pleased and relied on competing claims of domestic jurisdiction, the result would likely be serious conflict. If an upstream country builds a hydroelectric facility on a river that a downstream country relies on for drinking water and other uses, both countries will need to find a creative principle that facilitates friendly relations between them *and* permits them to meet the needs of their citizens. In 1960, the World Bank finalized a landmark agreement between India and Pakistan—two countries that frequently regarded each other as enemies—regarding use of the waters of the Indus River, whose waters both countries depend on for crucial irrigation. Not only did they divide water use equitably, but they also set up a permanent joint commission to oversee river uses, projects, and any disputes that might arise. By resolving this conflict amicably, both countries attracted a much-needed financial and infrastructure investment that had been held up by the Indus waters problem.

The resulting Indus Waters Treaty was so innovative and respected that it actually set a *new standard* for countries that need to find ways of equitably sharing the waters of international rivers. The treaty has survived well, despite subsequent wars and tension between India and Pakistan. Both countries feel that the treaty was a fair resolution, despite the other problems that plague their relations. In fact, it is the only agreement between these two countries that they have *consistently* upheld.

Since criteria help us persuade each other of the fairness of various options, it is important to let yourself see the merit of persuasive criteria even when they are not the ones you have chosen. In this sense, negotiators do not have to own the criteria; rather, criteria should be seen as shared assets that serve everyone involved. Also, remember that you may need to call upon various criteria for different issues in a dispute. "Yes, Charles, I can see how you calculated my car repair bill, since, as you note, the standard labor rate for those kinds of transmission repairs, under Massachusetts law, is $40 an hour. I have no argument with that. My concern is with the number of hours your mechanic spent on the job, which is typically four hours according to the standard aftermarket repair manual for my Volvo."

The following statements flow from some of the more common categories of criteria—law, precedent, similar cases, third-party evaluation, and market prices.

CRITERIA STATEMENT	CATEGORY OF CRITERIA
• In Kansas, unless an employer and employee agree otherwise, the employee's status is at-will.	Law
• We have paid previous babysitters $9 per hour.	Precedent
• Three companies that provide research on the biotech industry suggest that people doing this type of work make between $70,000 and $90,000 per year.	Research on similar cases
• Although it is generally the case that the Blue Book is a reliable indicator of a car's worth, we also need to look at the cost of upgrades for this particular model since it has had a lot of custom work.	Third-party evaluation plus market prices

In adversarial bargaining, people often attempt to close a negotiation by getting *what they prefer* from among the available options (with little or no regard for the needs of other parties). They assert various kinds of power—manipulation, willpower, stubbornness, "psyching" the other negotiator out, wielding threats, or outright lying or misrepresentation. This is an arbitrary approach to persuasion: one person's preferences are being imposed on another. Criteria, on the other hand, represent a fairer source of power in a negotiation—the power of legitimacy. This is because criteria tend to be more *objective*, or less subject to the control or influence of the parties themselves. When you use criteria to be persuasive about what constitutes a fair option, your leverage comes from having criteria that are persuasive to both parties and communicating that mutual fairness to your negotiating partners.

The following table compares a *subjective* willpower approach to decision making to an *objective* criteria approach.

WILLPOWER: SUBJECTIVE STATEMENTS	CRITERIA: OBJECTIVE STATEMENTS
• We're your biggest customer. You *need* our business. • I've got all day to wait for you to come around. I don't need to come to you. • I can take my business to any number of other vendors.	• Your company normally provides discounts of 10 percent or more to accounts that purchase more than 10,000 units. • Last year, you sold us those units for $27 each. • Your competitors are now offering the units for $26.

The following scenario deals with some of the criteria used in an auto purchase situation. Read these criteria, and then try coming up with additional ones.

SCENARIO

Jordon is negotiating with Frances, the owner of a used fire-engine-red 1997 Porsche Boxster. Jordon does his homework, finding different criteria for what the sale price should be.

CAR PURCHASE CRITERIA   *VALUE*

PRICE

• Similar Porsches in newspaper ads	$39,000–$49,000
• Blue Book retail	$46,000
• Blue Book trade-in	$38,000
• Car when new	$62,000
• Web site ads	$37,000–$45,000
• Local dealerships	$40,000–$51,000

FACTORS AFFECTING PRICE

• Miles on Porsche	12,000
• Accessories: sports package, special automatic transmission	$4,000
• Two years left on warranty	$1,000
• Condition	Excellent

Additional Criteria

_____

_____

_____

_____

_____

_____

SMART NEGOTIATOR TIP

Understand the Power of Scarcity

Scarcity is a very powerful principle that affects negotiation. Whether it's comic books, coins, antiques, or artwork, rarity affects the perception of value. When you are negotiating, you are constantly using criteria to emphasize the uniqueness of your asset or, conversely, the similarity of the asset to the competition, the walkaway, or the no-agreement alternative. Commonly we see this in the world around us, as salespeople and marketers emphasize that supply is limited, or this is the last one we have when it comes to cars, apartments, and so on.

In a basketball player contract negotiation, the agent wants to emphasize the scarcity of the player by noting statistical accomplishments and data to show different demographics appeal. The team focuses on how other available free agents can fulfill team needs as well or better.

Social psychologist Robert Cialdini in his book *Influence: The Psychology of Persuasion* identifies two sources for the power of scarcity. The first is that people take shortcuts to evaluating. Things that are more challenging to obtain are considered better than things that are easy to obtain. The second source is that when something cannot be possessed, people lose freedom or choice, and people generally hate to lose the freedom they already have. Psychological reactance theory says that when free choice is reduced, the reaction is to retain those freedoms or the item or service associated with this freedom.

When negotiating, use data that reveal the scarcity of your assets at play in negotiations. When the other party shares information emphasizing uniqueness or exclusivity, recognize the psychological phenomenon, and don't let it overly affect you.

SUMMARY

- Criteria serve as objective means to filter or narrow options.
- Criteria can defuse a negotiator's willpower or threats as a way of moving toward agreement.

- Explaining the outcome to someone outside the negotiation is easier when criteria have been established.
- Jointly creating a benchmark can help when no criteria are readily available.
- Criteria serve as leverage and help you advocate in negotiation.
- In preparation, focusing on criteria that is persuasive to the other party will help you reach an agreement.

QuickGuide: Criteria

Definition	Criteria are the precedents, benchmarks, and standards used by negotiators to evaluate their options.
Importance	Criteria help parties feel fairly treated rather than taken advantage of, and can help parties defend their decisions.
Preparation	Research criteria to filter and alter the options and help move the negotiation toward closure.
Dialogue	Question: "Before we decide on adding a new product line, what's the latest data from the trial programs on the West Coast?"
	Statement: "My goal is to be treated fairly by using objective standards to help both of us make a decision."
Tips	Ask for criteria. Try to raise criteria that are persuasive to both sides. Focus first on understanding the standards of the other side. If its standards do not fit the situation, show understanding and then distinguish the current situation.

YOUR NEGOTIATION WORKSHEET

Consider your own negotiation again. Reflect on your interests from the previous chapter and write down possible criteria. If you can't access that information right now, write down the categories or sources of rationale such as market data, previous practices, or legal standards, and you can research the data later. After generating criteria, check those that may be persuasive to the *other* party in your negotiation.

Your Negotiation Worksheet

Criteria	Persuasive?

REVIEW (*SEE ANSWER KEY AT END OF CHAPTER*)

Check all that apply

1. What are criteria?
   __ a) Objective standards
   __ b) Data a neutral third party would use to determine what's fair
   __ c) The negotiation element on which most time should be spent
   __ d) Factors like market rates and past precedents between the parties

2. According to Cialdini, what are two sources for the power of scarcity?
___ a) People prefer control to freedom.
___ b) People do not like scarce things.
___ c) People take shortcuts to evaluating.
___ d) People generally hate to lose the freedoms they have.

Is the statement conveying interests or criteria?

1. My concern about the noise from your apartment or any other is that I need to be able to sleep restfully and not be awakened in the middle of the night.
2. Let's check with the landlord to see what the noise policy is.
3. I just want to be treated fairly here. I want to be treated like any other tenant would be treated.

True or False

___ 1. There can be no disputes over criteria.
___ 2. Criteria and standards are among the most powerful ways to persuade your negotiation partners that an option is fair for all.
___ 3. Criteria are always readily available.
___ 4. Criteria must be known and understood before the parties can make progress.
___ 5. You can consider criteria only with the other parties present.
___ 6. Criteria help you defend—to yourself and others—the outcome of a negotiation.

ANSWER KEY

Check all that apply

1. What are criteria?
   a) Yes. The fundamental definition of criteria involves objective standards.
   b) Yes. Fair and neutral data are an example of criteria.

c) No. In most negotiations I generally recommend spending more time on interests and options because these help create more value. In many situations criteria may not be available or will not advance the negotiation. When research or precedent is the determining factor for closing a negotiation, the parties will need to discover, share, and discuss the legitimate criteria to make a decision.

d) Yes. Market rates and past precedents serve as criteria.

2. According to Cialdini, what are two sources for the power of scarcity?

___ a) No. Cialdini did not cite preference for control over freedom as a source of the power of scarcity. In fact, he points toward the dislike of losing freedom as a source of scarcity's impact.

___ b) No. This states the opposite of the scarcity phenomenon.

___ c) Yes. One source of scarcity's power is that people take shortcuts to evaluating. Things that are more challenging to obtain are considered better than things that are easy to obtain.

___ d) Yes. A second source of scarcity's power is that people generally hate to lose the freedoms they have. When free choice is reduced, the reaction is to retain those freedoms or the item or service associated with those freedoms.

Is the statement conveying interests or criteria?

1. Interests. Words like "needs" and "concerns" generally convey interests.
2. Criteria. The general policy of the building is being asked for.
3. Interests and criteria. This is a tougher one. The person's interest is in adhering to fairness or criteria. To meet that interest, he or she could bring up criteria such as specific precedents—that is, how other tenants are treated.

True or False

1. False. There are sometimes disputes over which standards of criteria are most applicable. These, too, can be resolved by negotiating.

2. True. Criteria and standards *are* powerful ways to persuade.

3. False. Criteria are *not* always available. Sometimes you have to look hard for them, or create fair mechanisms.

4. False. While having criteria generally helps, generating interests and options usually leads to the greatest progress.

5. False. You should invest some time in researching standards and criteria that will be persuasive to you, your "internal" audience (spouse, boss, kids, etc.), and your negotiating partners.

6. True. Audiences and other critics (including yourself) may be much more persuaded by criteria.

3

Options: Brainstorm Creatively

Options *are possible solutions to satisfy interests. They are possibilities that parties agree or say yes to.*

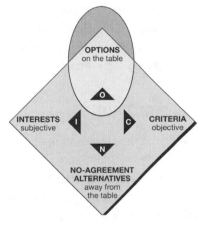

THE CHALLENGE

In 1996, relations between the San Diego Teachers Association and the San Diego City School District were spiraling downward. There had been numerous demonstrations of anger and personal attacks at meetings. The traditional concessional bargaining process used by the union and district administrators was simply not working. In February, negotiations imploded, and the teachers' union called members to strike. The strike lasted five anguished days before the union and management announced a settlement. Parents, taxpayers, and the business community were vocal about their disgust with the situation. Parents formed their own union, charges of racism were leveled at parties, and people on all sides felt attacked, victimized, and hurt.

In 1998, parties returned to the table for a new round of contract negotiations. One especially difficult topic was what to do about underperforming schools, which had a myriad of problems including poor performance on standardized testing. The difficulty was that the positions of teachers and administrators seemed far apart. Management historically asked for merit pay for teachers working at underperforming schools. The union said "no merit pay" and would not talk about the issue further. Using traditional negotiation methods, the conversation would have ended there.

The situation was exacerbated by the fact that the activist parents who had formed a "union" were outraged that underperforming schools were being ignored, citing race and class concerns. Some parents demanded to be at the collective bargaining table so their voices could be heard.

THE SOLUTION

In the 1990s, labor and management parties increasingly sought more collaborative problem-solving approaches for labor relations. Following the 1996 strike, the San Diego Teachers Association and management turned to this approach for their 1998 contract talks. While the negotiation teams did not give in to parents' demands to be seated at the negotiation table, they heard the importance and urgency of their voices.

Both sides were able to acknowledge their shared problems and articulate their common interests to each other. They recognized that underperforming schools were hard to staff, meaning that they had chronically high turnover rates, leading to a disproportionate percentage of new and inexperienced teachers in those schools. "We [had] something like 2,000 new teachers who needed support and assistance," said Marc Knapp, president of the teachers' union. Experts say that there is a positive correlation between teacher experience and student performance.

After a good deal of brainstorming, the parties came up with the concept of a mentorship program. Experienced teachers would be able to apply for three-year mentorships and agree to transfer to a hard-to-staff school and work with new teachers. The mentor teachers were given $4,500 in additional pay per year and the option of a second three-year mentorship. Both sides knew they would be criticized for not providing mentor programs at all schools, but, in the words of one union representative, "We had to put the limited funds to the best use, and we had to do something about these specific schools because if we didn't, these negotiations would just have been another waste of time."

San Diego City Schools superintendent Bertha Pendleton was thrilled with the solution. "Our mentor teachers have invaluable experience that can be focused on helping these schools improve student achievement. The amazing thing is that neither side had these ideas in mind before negotiations started."

On April 1, 1998, after three months of intense negotiating, the parties agreed to the terms of a new three-year contract. This was the first time in the school district's history that the two sides signed a contract before the previous one had expired. The contract was praised as fiscally responsible and fair. Parents who had protested loudly now stood and cheered the innovative solutions to improve teaching at the most difficult schools.

Source: Maureen Magee, "Schools, Teachers Agree on Quick Pact/San Diego Strike Memories Help Prompt Accord," *San Diego Union-Tribune*, April 2, 1998.

Overview: OPTIONS

Focusing on Options

- Generates more creative solutions
- Enables parties to satisfy their interests better
- Creates the Best Possible Agreement

Bottom Line

Options provide the answers in a negotiation.
They can be the joint solutions to shared problems.

The San Diego schools story helps us understand one of the most powerful ways that negotiators expand the pie in negotiations: They create solutions that are "outside the box." By truly understanding the interests involved, you can brainstorm many options that satisfy these interests. That is, if you know the underlying needs and desires of both parties, you can generate multiple solutions to meet them. In the ICON Value Diamond, options are the possible solutions that parties might ultimately agree to. They are pieces of a proposal or offer that you agree to in order to resolve the negotiation. But I recommend that you don't jump to options first. If you don't fully understand the interests of all the parties, you are ill-equipped to find the best solution. That's why spending time discovering and discussing interests sets the stage for good options. Having a solid grasp of criteria will allow you to propose options that are reasonable and advocate for your own and shared interests.

Let's return to the negotiation between Helen Hoops and the Golden Gaters for a moment. By looking at each party's interests, many options can be put on the table. Helen's agent and the team manager can come up with numerous options on the issues of compensation, responsibilities, perks, terms, and conditions. In this context, "issues" are the specific points, questions, or categories that are to be discussed in a negotiation.

Options that satisfy shared interests or meet both sides' interests are the ones most likely to be agreed upon. After all, unilateral options come across as positions. Helen wants to reduce her tax liability this year, while the team wants to limit its fixed costs. Paying Helen a deferred bonus or a higher salary in later years are options that could meet both parties' interests. These options and a few others are listed in the box on the next page.

And what about the restaurant team of Darrin and Wayman? Simply finding more time to communicate with each other or share expectations and frustrations more openly could lead to a solution to their negotiation. Prioritizing their interests would be a helpful first step. Based on what we know, one of the options they could look at might include more ownership for Darrin in exchange for a larger role in day-to-day management for Wayman.

All parties in a negotiation should prepare by brainstorming possible options and carefully reviewing what they might agree to. During the negotiation, the parties will be trying to reach a great agreement—what I call the Best Possible Agreement (BPA). The BPA is the ultimate win-win solution—the optimal solution for all negotiating parties. It is the option or package of options that expands the pie the most and provides the most objectively fair outcome. Preparing the BPA before you negotiate and aiming for this as a target keeps you focused on creating value. People tend to be more successful if they have a clear picture of what they're aiming for. If the parties truly understand the ICON elements of their negotiation, they can craft a deal to serve everyone's needs exceptionally well. The BPA may be sketchy when you begin, but it will evolve as you learn more about each other's interests. Continually envision and even discuss what an ideal agreement will look like for all parties. Remember that using a range for quantifiable issues can be helpful, and that some creative options won't be uncovered until you've actually started the negotiation.

Options for Signing Helen to the Team

Issue 1: Financial Compensation

- Deferred bonuses and/or salary
- Flat rate or base salary plus incentives
- Bonuses based on games played, all-star appearances, MVP recognition, points scored, and rebounds

Issue 2: Responsibilities

- Player-coach role for Helen
- Get Helen her own TV/radio show

Issue 3: Perks

- More comp tickets
- Personal massage therapist in locker room

Issue 4: Terms and Conditions

- No-trade clause
- Mix of guaranteed/nonguaranteed compensation
- Exit clauses
- 2–3 year deal

Issue 5: Other

- Hire Helen's dad, Harry, as coach

In the Helen Hoops negotiation, suppose Helen and her agent, Monique, develop a BPA that reflects the maximum value possible from their perspective:

Helen's Estimate of Best Possible Agreement

- Two-year agreement:
  Year 1: $1.3–$1.6 million
  Year 2: $1.5–$2.0 million
- $250,000–$500,000 signing bonus deferred until year two
- $50,000–$75,000 MVP bonus
- $25,000–$50,000 all-star bonus
- No trade, except with Helen's approval
- Weekly TV-radio show
- Team captain and spokesperson
- No motorcycling for Helen during term of contract

Note that using ranges in your BPA instead of firm dollar amounts will prevent the BPA from becoming a position. Tying ranges to criteria (in this case, performance) can be helpful, too. Beginning with ranges can also help prevent haggling.

It is also important to know your Minimum Possible Agreement (MPA)—your "bottom line," although not just in the economic sense. Your MPA is the list of elements required by you in any agreement. There may come a point when you realize that reaching an agreement no longer makes sense because what's on the table contains less value than your MPA. This situation should serve as a trigger to consider using your no-agreement alternatives (see Chapter 4). Knowing these alternatives helps generate your MPA. It's important not to let your MPA close your mind or drive your behavior as you progress through your negotiation, however. Doing so can hinder your ability to reach an agreement because it often leads to positional behavior.

In the Helen Hoops negotiation, Helen and her agent, Monique, develop their MPA in order to know when to seriously consider walking away from the negotiation. Kerry West, general manger of the Golden Gaters, does the same. The MPAs of each party follow.

HELEN'S MPA

- One-year agreement
- $1.2 million salary (based on New York Turnkey's offer)
- Salary guarantee
- No-trade clause

GENERAL MANAGER'S MPA

- One-year agreement
- $1.5 million salary (based on their BATNA, Shaquilla Eaglesclaw)
- No motorcycling during term of contract

The following scenario offers you an opportunity to practice generating options.

SCENARIO

Christina is a renter in a duplex. She is also a professor at a nearby community college where she has a heavy teaching load. She lives on the top floor, and another renter, Brian, lives on the bottom floor. Brian likes to play the piano. He has been playing the piano in the late afternoon and early evening, which really bothers Christina because that's when she grades papers and exams and does her preparation for class. Christina and Brian talk. The early portion of their conversation focuses on interests.

Can you see any interests that Christina and Brian have in common? "Being a good/tolerant neighbor" might be a strong foundation—both parties might be willing to make reasonable adjustments to their current behaviors to please their neighbor. What options can you come up with? Create three options to meet the interests stated above. Compare your options to the sample ones on page 45.

CHRISTINA'S INTERESTS

- Concentrate on her work
- Not listen to music that she hates (rock music)
- Listen to music that she likes (classical)
- Be a tolerant neighbor

BRIAN'S INTERESTS

- Get better at the piano
- Be a good neighbor
- Exercise his creativity
- Feel in control of his time

Options

1.

_____

2.

_____

3.

_____

Are all options equally valuable in a negotiation? Yes and no. While the goal of brainstorming should be to creatively explore many options that might satisfy the shared and differing interests of parties, options that are a good fit have a higher likelihood of being adopted.

What prevents us from generating good solutions to problems? Occasionally we assume that *a* problem is really *their* problem. So thought the seasoned old admiral aboard an aircraft carrier who noticed a light ahead in the night. "This is the aircraft carrier *Defiance*," he radioed. "Adjust your position." A young voice radioed back and politely suggested that the admiral adjust the course of his vessel. Indignant, the admiral replied, "Young man, this is an aircraft carrier, and I am an admiral. Adjust your course immediately!" The sheepish voice radioed back: "Sir, this is a lighthouse. Recommend you adjust course as soon as possible."

The admiral committed several errors of judgment. He assumed that he could impose a solution by "pulling rank." He also assumed that the problem and its solution were entirely the responsibility of someone else. In fact, their urgent problem was a shared one. A collision would have been in no one's interest!

Sample Options for Brian and Christina

1. Brian gets Christina's schedule and avoids playing the piano when she is home.
2. Brian practices his classical music (but not other styles of music) when Christina is home.
3. Christina calls Brian when the music is bothering her.
4. Brian moves his piano to the sunroom at the back of the house because Christina does not spend much time above Brian's sunroom.
5. Christina lends Brian her synthesizer keyboard, which plays just like a piano, has a headset, and produces no external sound.

Many negotiations can be resolved more efficiently by understanding this simple lesson. Shared problems require building shared solutions—options—that are directly linked to the interests of all parties involved in a negotiation.

Another barrier to effective negotiation occurs when we assume that our task as negotiators is simply to grab as much as we can. This belief comes from the mistaken assumption that, "Whatever they get, I lose, so I have to grab a lot, and grab quickly." In fact, it is essential to create value first—as much as possible—and then talk about fair and equitable ways to divide it. This is "expanding the pie." The best negotiators use the power of generating many options to satisfy as many needs as possible for the parties. Options, in this sense, are the tool you use to expand the pie.

Asked and Answered

No Options

Sometimes there are no options that are agreeable. You may be negotiating with someone who is very inflexible, or within a framework with no room for discussion. In this case, consider your BATNA—your Best Alternative to a Negotiated Agreement. Discussing your BATNA can be a powerful tool in negotiating. And going to your BATNA—walking away from the negotiating table—may serve your interests better than making a bad agreement. BATNAs are discussed in more detail in Chapter 4.

SMART NEGOTIATOR TIP

Use Risk to Create Better Options

When people can potentially gain something, they will generally prefer a sure thing over risk. When people can potentially lose something, they will generally prefer risk over a sure thing. Consider a plaintiff and defendant in a trial. All things being equal, a plaintiff would more likely choose settlement over trial because of the defendant's aversion to risk. The reverse would be true for defendants who would rather go to trial than settle because of their desire for risk over pain.

Kahneman and Tversky pioneered research showing risk-aversion preference for those with something to gain and risk-seeking preference for those with something to lose: 84 percent of study participants preferred a smaller sure gain over chance of a somewhat larger gain; 87 percent of study participants preferred taking a risk over accepting a certain loss.

When negotiating, find ways to provide certainty when your negotiation counterparts have something to gain and risk when they have potential pain. When crafting options, you should consider more concrete certain proposals for gains and options that allow the other side to "gamble" rather than be met with a sure loss.

SUMMARY

- Options are possible solutions to satisfy interests.
- Creative options expand the pie.
- Options can be tailored to meet the interests related to each issue of a negotiation.
- Spending time brainstorming generates more creative options.
- The Best Possible Agreement (BPA) is the package of options that best meets the parties' interests.
- The Minimum Possible Agreement (MPA) is the least satisfactory package of options a party can agree to.

- Focusing on generating options develops a joint problem-solving approach, which builds shared solutions.
- Seeking possibly agreeable options as you prepare helps you reach an agreement.

QuickGuide: Options

Definition	Options are possible solutions to satisfy interests. Some of these options will later become part of the final agreement.
Importance	Finding options that satisfy interests creates a higher likelihood of achieving an agreement.
Preparation	Come up with many options that might satisfy the shared, differing, and conflicting interests of the parties.
Dialogue	Question: "What are some possible ways to meet your need for quality?"
	Statement: "I'm sure there are a lot of different ways we could go here. These are a few of my thoughts on what we could do. I'm not asking you to commit—let's just brainstorm together first and decide later."
Tips	Ask for a range of ideas. Focus first on general concepts rather than specific details. Share options without making demands. Don't say yes or no to anything initially.

YOUR NEGOTIATION WORKSHEET

Let's return now to *your* negotiation. Review the criteria you wrote in the last chapter and then brainstorm some options on the worksheet that follows. After you have brainstormed, evaluate. Check options that make up the Best Possible Agreement. Then check options that make up the Minimum Possible Agreement.

Your Negotiation Worksheet

Options	BPA	MPA

(Check options that serve as part of BPA and/or MPA.)

REVIEW (*SEE ANSWER KEY AT END OF CHAPTER*)

Check all that apply

1. What is an option?
   __ a) A single solution that is presented as the right answer for agreement
   __ b) A clue to a person's underlying interests
   __ c) An objective standard, benchmark, or precedent
   __ d) The specific category or question to be discussed in a negotiation

2. What is an issue?
   __ a) A need or desire of a party in a negotiation
   __ b) A possible solution

___ c) A specific category or question to be discussed in a negotiation

___ d) A demand that a party makes

3. What is the Best Possible Agreement (BPA)?
___ a) The optimal option from your perspective
___ b) The ultimate solution for all the negotiating parties
___ c) A solution developed by generating options and crafting
an agreement that expands the pie the most
___ d) A target used to stay focused on creating value
___ e) An agreement on an issue without final agreement until
the very end

4. What is the Minimum Possible Agreement (MPA)?
___ a) An option that is generated by looking at criteria and no-
agreement alternatives
___ b) An option that is similar to the bottom line
___ c) An option that pertains only to economic issues
___ d) An option that provide a trigger point for using your
no-agreement alternatives
___ e) Options that are different for each party

Is the questioner looking for interests or options?

1. What do you care about?
2. How can we as doctors help meet the patients' demands for our
time?
3. What are some ways we can distribute the work?
4. Why is a product small and light enough to carry in your brief-
case important to you?
5. Now that we know what we're trying to achieve, let's brainstorm specific roles and responsibilities for each of us. We need
to get more concrete now.

Is the questioner looking for interests, options, or criteria?

1. What are some ways we can get to Boston from here?
2. What does the firm usually do in these situations?
3. Regarding your employment agreement, how do other departments within the company handle noncompetition clauses?
4. Given that this is the result of a mix-up on both ends, what are some different solutions to solve this problem?

True or False

____1. Positions are the underlying desires or wants of the parties. Demands are the solutions to meet those desires or wants.

____2. A position is one possible option.

____3. Options are not intended to satisfy the parties' interests.

ANSWER KEY

Check all that apply

1. What is an option?
   a) Yes. This is both an option and a position. Remember that a position is a demand fixated on one option.
   b) Yes. Options meet interests. Knowing the option gives insight into the underlying interests.
   c) No. This is the definition of criteria.
   d) No. This is the definition of an issue. Within each issue there may be various options.

2. What is an issue?
   a) No. This is the definition of an interest. Within each issue there may be various interests.
   b) No. This is the definition of an option.
   c) Yes. This is the definition of an issue.
   d) No. This is the definition of a position. There may be a position on any given issue.

3. What is the Best Possible Agreement (BPA)?
    a) No. The BPA is the optimal package of options from the per-
        spectives of all negotiating parties. This is, of course, subject
        to a range of possibilities. It is an attempt to be as fair and
        objective as possible.
    b) Yes. The BPA is the ultimate solution for all negotiation par-
        ties. See answer (*a*).
    c) Yes. Combining and adjusting options is necessary to craft a
        package that expands the pie the most.
    d) Yes. Having some idea of an optimal solution will help keep
        the attention and focus on creating value rather than giving in
        to the tendency to only divide things up.
    e) No. Reaching agreement on an issue without final agreement
        until the very end is the definition of a tentative agreement.
        This is discussed in Chapter 7.

4. What is the Minimum Possible Agreement (MPA)?
    a) Yes. A primary way to generate an MPA is to use criteria and
        no-agreement alternatives.
    b) Yes. An MPA is similar to a bottom line because it serves as
        a trigger point to walk away from the negotiation. See answer
        (c) for differentiation.
    c) No. The bottom line is often seen as pertaining only to eco-
        nomic issues. MPA focuses on the entire agreement necessary
        to move forward.
    d) Yes. An MPA provides a trigger point to go to your no-agree-
        ment alternatives. Be careful, however, of focusing too much
        on the MPA and becoming positional in your negotiations.
    e) Yes. Each party has a separate MPA. However, different parties'
        MPAs may be similar in what issues must be agreed upon.

Is the questioner looking for interests or options?

1. Interests. The words "care about" often indicate interests.
2. Options. The person is seeking possible solutions to meet the
    patients' needs for more time.

3. Options. The person seeks possible solutions for distributing the work.
4. Interests. The questioner is requesting why meeting certain interests (small and light) are important. Understanding the prioritization of interests may help create better options.
5. Options. When parties are trying to be more "concrete" and take specific action steps by agreeing to specific roles and responsibilities, they are looking for options.

Is the questioner looking for interests, options, or criteria?

1. Options. The person is asking for different ways or options for getting to Boston.
2. Criteria. Precedent is being asked for. Of course, the criteria can be transformed into an option for how to resolve the situation.
3. Criteria. The person is asking for employment contract standards in other parts of the company.
4. Options. The person is attempting to get some brainstormed possibilities to resolve the situation.

True or False

1. False. Interests are the underlying desires or wants. Options are the solutions that satisfy those desires and wants. Note that if you ask for "wants" and "desires," you may get options rather than interests. A party wants or desires that his or her interests be met *and* that the options he or she prefers be agreed to. Like an iceberg where the largest portion is beneath the water, interests are often hidden from sight.
2. True. A position is really just one possible option. Of course, positions are presented as the *only* way to satisfy the interest. An option is *one* possible way to satisfy the interest.
3. False. Options are possible solutions that are crafted to meet various interests.

No-Agreement Alternatives:
Know Your BATNA

No-Agreement Alternatives *are the self-help possibilities of each party if no agreement is reached. BATNA (the Best Alternative to a Negotiated Agreement) is the no-agreement alternative that best meets the party's interests.*

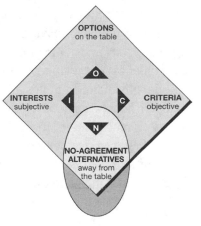

THE CHALLENGE

Gene, Molly, and their two children live together in a two-bedroom house. They are expecting another child in four months, so they decide to look for a new house to get more space. They find a beautiful four-bedroom rambler that seems ideal. It's in a great neighborhood with a well-regarded school system. At the open house, Gene whispers to Molly, "This is it. This is our dream house." The entire family gets excited. Gene and Molly fret over their bid, over securing a mortgage, and over moving. They stop looking for other houses. They place a bid. It gets rejected. They place a second bid. It gets rejected. After the second bid is rejected, Molly and

Gene talk. Gene says, "I'm feeling really stuck. I feel like we have to get this house." Molly replies, "I know what you mean. I feel like we have no choices."

THE SOLUTION

Molly and Gene take a step back. "You know," says Molly, "maybe we should ask ourselves what to do if we don't get this house. That's a worst-case scenario we haven't wanted to look at. Maybe we need to look at that now." Gene sighs and says, "You're right. As much as I don't want to face that possibility, let's think about it."

They discuss staying at their current home. While they had not previously investigated making additions or remodeling, they decide to talk to an architect and contractor. Gene and Molly also realize that they made a mistake by not continuing to look at other houses. They had become emotionally attached to this dream house. They spend the weekend going to open houses again. Surprisingly, they find another house they like nearly as much and in the same price range.

They then decide to put in another bid on the rambler that includes a deadline for agreement and contingencies like passing an inspection. They had not included this in earlier bids and had felt anxious about it,

---

Overview: NO-AGREEMENT ALTERNATIVES

Negotiating Using No-Agreement Alternatives

- Helps you prepare for a negotiation by clearly defining how far you're willing to go—your Minimum Possible Agreement (or bottom line)
- Gives you a backup plan
- Helps prevent over- or underestimating the other party's negotiating position

Bottom Line

No party should agree to something that is worse than their Best Alternative to a Negotiated Agreement (their BATNA).

although they did not admit it to each other. Now that they have two real alternatives to the dream house, Gene and Molly feel more confident in the negotiation. They realize that they can walk away from the first house and still have something good to walk away to. They know they would be okay with the outcome no matter how it turned out. Gene and Molly, in effect, have realized the potential of their no-agreement alternatives.

No-agreement alternatives are the walkaway possibilities each party has if no agreement is reached. They do not require the other side's agreement. As a matter of fact, we define them as the actions you take if you don't reach agreement at all. In general, no party should agree to something that is worse than their Best Alternative to a Negotiated Agreement, or BATNA—the concept made famous in *Getting to Yes*. Your BATNA is the alternative that meets your interests best. Here is a simple illustration of how no-agreement alternatives can work when you are buying or selling a car:

THE PROSPECTIVE BUYER GOES TO A CAR DEALERSHIP

Buyer's No-Agreement Alternatives: How else will the buyer satisfy his interests in getting to work reliably if he cannot come to an agreement with the seller?

- Buy a car from another dealer
- Buy a car through the classifieds
- Get a bus pass
- Buy a car at the local auto show
- Join a carpool
- Walk

Seller's No-Agreement Alternatives: How else will the seller satisfy her interests in making a commission and achieving her sales goals if she cannot come to an agreement with the buyer?

- Sell the car to someone else
- Sell a different car to a different buyer
- Ask her manager to adjust her sales goals downward

In nonnegotiation settings, the words "options" and "alternatives" are often used interchangeably. In the ICON negotiation model, these words are used very differently. Options are "on-the-table" ideas that the parties can agree to together. In a car-buying situation, options include the amount of the down payment, the color of the car, the trade-in allowance, and so on. No-agreement alternatives are what parties do on their own if no agreement is reached between the parties as a matter of self-help. They are done "away" from the table. Options are what the parties say yes to. No-agreement alternatives are what the parties do if they say no to each other.

What will Helen Hoops and the Golden Gaters do if they cannot reach an acceptable agreement with each other? Here is a sample of their no-agreement alternatives:

HELEN'S NO-AGREEMENT ALTERNATIVES	TEAM'S NO-AGREEMENT ALTERNATIVES
• Sign with another team—the New York Turnkeys (Helen's BATNA)	• Sign one of the top free agents instead, such as Shaquilla Eaglesclaw (team's BATNA)
• Go to the Asian or European pro leagues	• Use the reserve center, Svetlana Nater, instead of Helen
• Retire	• Draft Ma Jian, the top center from the Chinese League's Shanghai Jets
• Change career to coach or broadcaster	

As you can see, some no-agreement alternatives are better than others. Helen's BATNA is signing with the Portland Trail Lasers because they are closer to her home in the San Francisco Bay Area, they have made her a fair offer, and their team made it to the championship round last year. Of her several no-agreement alternatives, this one meets her interests the best. The Golden Gaters' BATNA is signing Shaquilla Eaglesclaw because she is emerging as a top center and would meet the team's needs.

Another example of BATNAs in action is the sales ritual at street fairs or bazaars. Buyers in these venues frequently make moves to walk away from vendors at a certain point in negotiations. What happens to the offering price as the potential buyer starts walking? In most cases, the price starts falling sharply as the vendor asks the buyer to come to her senses and take the bargain. The buyer is pulling an invisible BATNA lever, demonstrating that she can walk away at any moment because she is confident of getting a better deal from another vendor. In a bazaar, you don't have to do much research on prices because the number of other shops and stands means that somebody else may be able to meet your price.

A classic mistake in most negotiations, as we saw from the Gene and Molly home-purchase story, is to fail to consider your no-agreement alternatives in advance. In order to come to the table fully prepared for any outcome, you must do your homework on your BATNA. Thinking critically about the actual or possible BATNA of the other parties is never a waste of time either, although you must be careful not to over- or underestimate any parties' no-agreement alternatives.

Here are four points to keep in mind when preparing your no-agreement alternatives and BATNA:

1. **Reexamine your interests.** What are other ways of addressing them without reaching an agreement with the party who will be at the table with you? For example, consider Andrew, who is negotiating with his manager, Chris, over a salary increase and promotion:

    ### Andrew's interests
    - Save money to go to graduate school
    - Be treated fairly
    - Increase level of professional development before going back to school
    - Take a vacation this year
    - Make sure salary keeps pace with inflation
    - Learn from and be challenged by work

    ### Andrew's no-agreement alternatives
    - Get a job offer from another company
    - Transfer to a different department in same company
    - Transfer to a company office in another city
    - Apply to graduate school and get loans
    - Quit job and travel
    - Sell car
    - Reduce other expenses
    - Move back home
    - See a career counselor
    - Take a second job

2. **Select your BATNA.** Once you have brainstormed some no-agreement alternatives, consider which of these meet your interests best. If Andrew's highest-priority interest is professional development and being challenged, then looking for another job may be his BATNA.

3. **Improve your BATNA.** Prior to going into a negotiation, make an effort to improve your no-agreement alternatives. For example, in Andrew's situation, if getting another job offer is his BATNA, then looking through the want ads, calling people in his network, setting up interviews, and perhaps even getting an offer makes his BATNA much more real than simply the knowledge that he could possibly get a job elsewhere.

4. **Estimate the other side's no-agreement alternatives.** In addition to figuring out your own no-agreement alternatives, it is important to at least estimate what the other party's might be. Estimate the other party's alternatives in order to gauge his or her desire for agreement. In many situations, you may never know what the other side's actual alternatives are. People may not disclose this information to you, particularly if they do not believe their BATNA is strong. However, by at least estimating what their alternatives might be, you begin to understand their perspective. And if they disclose their BATNA, you want to be prepared to address it knowledgeably, and perhaps be in a position to help them see that it's not as good as they think.

Here are a few more examples of no-agreement alternatives:

Imagine you are a management representative in a labor contract negotiation and are preparing for your session with the union president. You want to consider the president's alternatives to negotiating a contract with you, which might include:

- Strike
- Work slowdown
- Speak directly to consumers/public via media, advertising, protests
- Resign from presidency
- Cut you out of the loop and talk with other management negotiators

Imagine you are a pharmaceutical company representative and are preparing for a negotiation with the CEO of a biotech start-up. Your goal in this negotiation is to create a joint alliance with the start-up to produce and deliver to the market an innovative treatment for liver disease. Your company has the marketing and distribution channels as well as the financial clout. The biotech company has the compound for the new medication. Before you meet with the biotech's CEO, you want to consider her alternatives to negotiating the alliance deal with you, which might include:

- Attempt to take the liver disease treatment to the market on their own
- Find venture capital money
- Find a different partner company
- Sell foreign rights to other companies
- Sell all rights to the treatment to other companies

SMART NEGOTIATOR TIP

Watch for Overconfidence

When people become overconfident in their chance of success, it reduces the likelihood of agreement. For example, when lawyers prepare their cases against each other, they often begin believing that their cases are stronger than they actually are. As new evidence comes in, they start to filter and focus on what confirms their own beliefs. One or both sides see going to court, their no-agreement alternative, as being better than a judge might actually rule. As a result, when the two attorneys talk settlement, they face the challenge that beyond tactical motivations to bluff or oversell their case, the attorneys likely honestly evaluate their cases as better than they actually are which creates a bigger gap, making it more difficult to compromise.

Bazerman and Neale found in their research that negotiators see themselves as more honest, cooperative, and fair than others. They conducted research that showed lawyers in final-offer arbitration (each side submits a resolution with no further negotiation) overestimated the likelihood of success by 18 percent.

When you negotiate, reality-test how good your walkaway is. Ask a trusted colleague or a friend who can be objective about the strengths and weaknesses of your no-agreement alternatives. This will prevent you from feeling overconfident and will provide you with greater clarity so that you will ultimately make wiser choices.

SUMMARY

- No-agreement alternatives are the self-help possibilities if no agreement is reached.
- The Best Alternative to a Negotiated Agreement (BATNA) is the no-agreement alternative that best meets a party's interests.
- No-agreement alternatives are what each party does on his or her own "away from the table," while options are "on-the-table" possibilities that parties might agree to do together.
- You can develop your no-agreement alternatives, and ultimately your BATNA, by examining your interests.
- Looking for ways to improve your BATNA as you prepare enhances your ability to create a better agreement on the table.
- Estimating the other side's BATNA as you prepare will help you address it if they threaten to walk to it.

QuickGuide: No-Agreement Alternatives

Definition	No-agreement alternatives are the self-help possibilities each party has if no agreement is reached.
Importance	No-agreement alternatives help determine whether or not to agree. They provide a backup plan and increase confidence and competence at the negotiation table. They can also prevent overestimating or underestimating the other party's power in a negotiation.
Preparation	Generate no-agreement alternatives by looking at your interests. Compare your BATNA with the possible agreement you may be making with the other party. Develop your Minimum Possible Agreement (MPA) by analyzing your BATNA.
Dialogue	Question: "If we don't come to an agreement, what might you do instead?" Statement: "While it would not be my preference, I might have to go to our second choice because of time urgency."
Tips	Prepare your no-agreement alternatives. Improve your BATNA. Estimate the other side's BATNA. Use your BATNA to protect your self-interest and create the Best Possible Agreement (BPA).

YOUR NEGOTIATION WORKSHEET

Let's focus on your own negotiation again. List the no-agreement alternatives—yours and your estimate of theirs. It may be helpful to first refer to the interests worksheet you filled out earlier. Check the alternative in your list that meets your interests the best—your BATNA. Do the same in their list—identify their BATNA.

Your Negotiation Worksheet

No-Agreement Alternatives	BATNA
Yours	
Theirs	

REVIEW (*SEE ANSWER KEY AT END OF CHAPTER*)

Check all that apply

1. What is a no-agreement alternative?
   __ a) The bottom line or what you are willing to agree to with the party at the table in a worst-case scenario
   __ b) Not agreeing with the party and doing nothing
   __ c) Going to a different party to get your needs met
   __ d) Mutually agreeing to go to third-party dispute resolution—voluntary arbitration

Is the statement an option or a no-agreement alternative?

1. I know our first preference is to create a companywide agreement. Short of that we're willing to discuss an agreement with just your department.
2. We have another organization that we're going to work with instead of yours.
3. The two of us are at impasse here. I know you don't want me to, but I'm going to talk to your management.
4. We have decided to keep the status quo and not utilize your services at this time.
5. Okay, this is below my bottom line but I'll give in and accept your offer.

ANSWER KEY

Check all that apply

1. What is a no-agreement alternative?
   a) No. Even if it's a worst-case scenario, if you agree with the other party, then this is an option rather than a no-agreement alternative.
   b) Yes. Doing nothing is a no-agreement alternative.
   c) Yes. If you do not agree with the party at the table and go to someone else, this is a no-agrecmcnt altcrnative.
   d) No. Even though an arbitrator is making a binding decision, the parties agreed to it voluntarily. Therefore, it is an option.

Is the statement an option or a no-agreement alternative?

1. Option. While it may not be this person's preferred option, both sides must still agree, which makes it an option.

2. No-agreement alternative. The person is stating they will *not* be coming to agreement.

3. No-agreement alternative. Going to management within the same organization without the other person's agreement is a no-agreement alternative. It might feel like an option because the parties are still within the same organization. Going to a *different* organization would also be a no-agreement alternative.

4. No-agreement alternative. Doing nothing for now is a no-agreement alternative. The other party's agreement is not necessary.

5. Option. Even though it may be below your bottom line, giving in and accepting the other side's offer is an agreement between the parties, and it is therefore an option.

PART TWO

THE 4D APPROACH

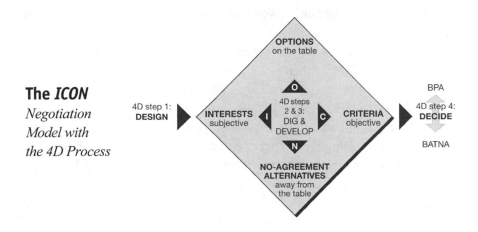

The *ICON*

*Negotiation
Model with
the 4D Process*

N egotiation can be absolutely frustrating when you don't have a game plan. You are about to decide something that may affect your career, family, or finances, but you have no idea how to approach the interaction let alone prepare effectively for it.

People who are successful at negotiating (and at most activities, for that matter) first visualize a target. Focusing on the four ICON elements—Interests, Options, Criteria, and No-Agreement Alternatives—as the initial target helps you map out the negotiation. But what comes next? How should you start the negotiation? Just knowing about ICON is helpful, but it may not be enough for success in a negotiation. You still need a strategy for action.

Part Two of this guide will provide you with such a strategy. I focus on what to actually *do* in a "live" negotiation. This is the *conducting* aspect of negotiations. It is the *how* of negotiation—how to put ICON into play in a collaborative manner. This is also where it gets harder. Simply knowing what to do is no guarantee that you will know how to do it.

While a lot of people may say that they negotiate on a win-win basis, it's not so easy to walk the talk.

In my experience, people sometimes claim that they want a win-win outcome but in fact are really looking for a situation in which *they* win *more* than you. The challenge of creating value for all parties becomes harder if any single person feels hurt, betrayed, or offended before, during, or after the negotiation. Win-win negotiating is much easier when there is trust between the parties. Once that trust is broken, the challenge is much greater. What is often characterized as miscommunication may have at its root a lack of trust.

When trust or communication falter, what we sometimes see is an instantaneous change of heart to "win-lose." Once this happens, how do you get the negotiations back on track? How do you ensure that your interests are met while preserving or creating a solid working relationship with others at the table? Win-lose thinking is often reactive and tactical, and does nothing to build the working relationship you need when negotiating things that really matter to you. Having a reliable strategic plan for negotiation helps you stay on course or find your way back if things don't go well. This is what the 4D approach offers.

THE 4D APPROACH

In the following chapters, you will discover the 4D strategic approach for negotiation. The 4D advice is precisely a strategy that helps build relationships and enhance communication as you negotiate toward better outcomes. This "how-to" section will advise you on the key steps to take in every phase of negotiation.

In these chapters I will give you my best advice on:

1. **DESIGN**: How to construct a negotiation from the beginning to prevent pitfalls and prepare parties for success
2. **DIG**: How to focus on interests
3. **DEVELOP**: How to craft creative practical options
4. **DECIDE:** How to come to agreement on individual issues and on the negotiation as a whole.

Step 1. Design: Frame the Negotiation

The 4D Design Step

is where you plan your negotiation approach. Careful design helps you avoid pitfalls and problems and helps you reach solutions.

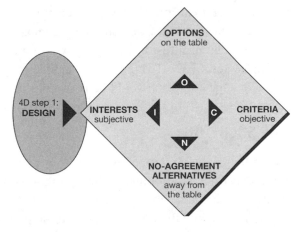

THE CHALLENGE

Linda McByte started Bugfree Software in her one-bedroom apartment in 1994. Within a year, Bugfree had grown to five employees. Within two years, Linda—now the CEO—had secured venture capital financing and issued an initial public offering (IPO). By 1999, Bugfree employed over 2,000 people nationwide, and its stock price had risen by 500 percent. Bugfree brought together its senior management from around the country once every quarter for eight hours in order to negotiate key strategic corporate issues. This was a very entrepreneurial group of young people who were accustomed to a wide-open approach to decision making. The agenda generally was not created until the day of the meeting. Invariably, the team members would never get through even one-third of the issues they planned to decide. Some critical issues would never get discussed. The meetings never started on time because so many managers arrived late or spent too much time catching up with each other once they did arrive. Once the meetings began, lots of time was spent just providing updates on new developments. No notes or minutes were taken or distributed. Many managers left the meetings feeling frustrated and unheard, believing they had solutions that no one was hearing or problems no one was paying attention to. Linda knew that the meetings were getting increasingly disorganized and ineffective.

While Bugfree's software programs were highly successful, Linda realized that their most important competitors were poised for a full assault on the market. One competing company with a great product had received a large infusion of capital, while another had recently hired a highly touted CEO. If Bugfree was unable to get its act together, Linda knew that the company would be in trouble soon.

THE SOLUTION

Linda began the next meeting by laying out in stark terms the reality of the competitive environment. She said that the way they worked in their quarterly meetings was unproductive and that they truly needed to act as a team. Linda and the others diagnosed the problem. Causes included the lack of an agreed-upon agenda, lack of facilitation, too many goals with too little time, and a lack of attention paid to critical issues and decisions. Ultimately, they realized that they needed to dramatically reduce the scope of their meetings. The team realized that the focus had to be on negotiating strategic issues.

They relegated the financial, legal, and operational issues to other meetings that would be facilitated by video and audio conferencing technology. They cut out the informational aspect of the meeting and set up an internal electronic newsletter to broadly communicate formal and informal news. They also planned an informal get-together dinner for the night preceding the monthly strategy meeting in order to provide time for vital socializing and relationship-building. The head of the organizational development department took on the role of meeting facilitator. An administrative assistant took notes on each meeting and work session and distributed summaries to senior management. Suggestions for the agenda were solicited a week before the meeting. The agenda itself was distributed electronically to all participants two days before the meeting.

As the meeting goals and the agenda became clearer, the group became more focused and better able to deal constructively with important issues, and consequently it was better able to make critical decisions on time.

Overview: THE DESIGN PHASE

Focusing on Design

- Helps you anticipate pitfalls and problems
- Decreases your susceptibility to difficult tactics
- Encourages interaction at the table and away from it

Bottom Line

Focusing on design increases the possibility of an agreement and also makes it easier to create value and come to closure.

The Bugfree example illustrates the importance of design in a meeting setting—of preparing a setting for effective and productive discussions. Without adequate preparation, there is no progress. The same is true for negotiations. In addition, effective design is necessary to make sure your efforts focus on the big picture—the best end-goal of a process. Consider this example:

> Imagine two large cities across the river from each other that have dreamed of building a bridge for decades. Finally, the cities get a federal grant and a bond issue. The very best construction company is chosen, and they sign a master contract to build the bridge. Because of parochialism and politics, however, the best designers are not chosen. The design studies misforecast the infrastructure necessary to accommodate future growth, the connection ramps are confusing, the

tollbooth setups are clogging, and the air and sound quality are problematic for both sides of the river. During both the impact assessment and construction phases, environmental groups sue to kill or modify the project. Even though the cities have the funds and a great construction company, the bridge is a disaster. It hastens the departure and damages the legacy of the mayors on both sides of the river. Wasted time, frustration, backtracking, confusion, and chaos reign in the resulting situation. Less than five years after finishing the bridge, the cities open discussions on building a new one to replace it.

What is the missing element in this scenario? Effective design. You must carefully *design* any structure before you build it. The Design step of negotiation is often underestimated or ignored entirely by negotiators. Typically, people begin negotiating by paying some degree of attention to social courtesies. Then one party jumps right into making offers. If the other party is awake, he or she will likely feel obligated to jump in with a counteroffer or bluff or balk. Unfortunately, this approach often rewards gamesmanship and stubbornness and reduces the possibility of agreement.

4D Key Point

Preparing for your negotiation will make all the difference.

What you do or don't do in the Design step of a negotiation can have tremendous influence on its outcome. Successfully completing the Design step establishes a frame for the negotiation and can help you avoid pitfalls, traps, and barriers, or take proactive steps to overcome them when they arise. Because negotiations are complex structures of relationships and communications, effective negotiators deliberately design the interaction.

4D Key Point

Until you create value, any price is too high.

Tactic Alert

The Haggle

Haggling happens when one party opens a negotiation by making an extreme or unreasonable offer and concedes sparingly while trying to obtain a more generous concession from you. Other tactics are sometimes used in combination with this one, such as "take it or leave it." Deal with the haggle by jointly discussing how to approach the negotiation (a preventive measure). Ask for interests early and often, and remember to share yours. Brainstorm options before evaluating them, and prepare your BATNA.

For situations where people want to jump right into offers, it may be useful to remember the following bit of advice: Until you create value, any price is too high. People may come into a negotiation ready to haggle. Make it clear that you want to focus on value by discussing interests first.

Aside from making negotiations more positive and adding more value, an effectively constructed and implemented Design step makes it easier to accomplish tasks at the heart of negotiation—the tasks of creating value and coming to closure. Later, I refer to these tasks in discussions of the Dig and Develop steps and then the Decide step.

DESIGN: "TEE IT UP" FOR SUCCESS

Consider the game of golf. Many golfers have rituals to tee up the ball and to be physically and mentally ready before they take a swing. They may carefully place their feet a specific distance from the ball, flex their knees, and take a certain number of practice swings. On putts, the golfer may walk around the hole and look carefully at the slope and line the ball will take. This initial investment in setting up paves the way for success.

Negotiation is more challenging than golf in at least one important sense: In negotiation, you must work *directly* with other people. You work *together* to kick off your negotiation journey, and the first few steps can get you going in the right direction or the wrong one.

There are three main tasks in the Design step:

1. Set goals
2. Construct an agenda
3. Deliver a core message.

These steps are discussed below.

Step 1: Set Goals

The most important task in the Design step is to identify your goals or objectives for a specific negotiation meeting. We consider two types of goals in negotiation: substance goals and relationship goals.

SUBSTANCE GOALS

Substance goals are the reason you are negotiating. The substance goal for a single meeting in a long negotiation process might be to get the parties to share interests, brainstorm options, propose a tentative agreement, or even sign a final agreement.

During the meeting, jointly confirm the goals for the meeting. Being explicit helps the parties get on the same page and drive toward common goals. If you are trying to reach a tentative decision, for example, remember to put the decision in writing in order to prevent later misunderstanding. This is the "what"—the piece of paper that tells you your goal has been reached. Drive toward this piece of paper and what it represents.

Let's return to the Helen Hoops negotiation. Helen's agent, Monique Lee, and Kerry West, the Golden Gaters' general manager, are sitting down at the table to begin negotiations. Kerry calls Monique and asks what she would like to accomplish in this first meeting. Monique says she wants both sides to share interests for the team and Helen.

In their second meeting, Kerry and Monique agree that they would like an initial proposal on the issues of responsibilities and conditions. For their third meeting, the two parties want to develop a proposal on the issues of compensation and perks. Fast-forward to the final meeting: Kerry and Monique have the goal of a signed agreement.

MEETING	SUBSTANCE GOAL
First	Share interests
Second	Joint proposal on responsibilities and conditions
Third	Joint proposal on compensation and perks
Final	Signed agreement

RELATIONSHIP GOALS

How will the parties in a negotiation relate to each other? How will they perceive one another when the negotiation is finished? Frame a clear goal for what you would *prefer* your relationship to be like. This gives the parties a target to focus on, regardless of whether you reach your substance goals or not. By focusing on the *preferred* working relationship between parties instead of taking this relationship for granted, you make it more possible to reach a collaborative outcome on the substance and also make future negotiations smoother.

Getting to Yes popularized the notion that negotiators should be "soft on the people and hard on the problem" when they negotiate. While this may imply that you should go easy on the people and your working relationships with them, it doesn't mean that you have to give in, even on relationship issues. It doesn't mean that you should avoid bringing up issues of how you are communicating or getting along. Indeed, you may need to be very assertive in order to build the kind of relationship you want. If you want to build a collaborative relationship and if doing so is not on the radar screen of your counterpart, you will have to work harder to achieve that goal.

Of course, relationships are two-way streets. The secret of strong relationship builders is that they persist in creating rapport and trust.

If the negotiation is to create a long-time partnership or alliance, then an important relationship goal might be to maintain collegial and respectful interactions. You might find it helpful at this stage to be open and candid—to make your assumptions, constraints, and expectations explicit. In later meetings, you can revisit your relationship goals at the beginning in order to keep things on track, and to summarize previous discussions to check what has been accomplished and what still needs to be done.

In the Helen Hoops negotiation, Monique has never worked with Kerry before because Kerry only recently became general manager. For the foreseeable future, Monique will be working with Kerry. They both have a relationship goal for their first meeting of establishing a pattern of collegiality and mutual respect.

Their first meeting goes poorly. A comment that Monique makes about the team's financial situation is misunderstood and upsets Kerry. The two agree that a relationship goal for their second meeting will lead to clearer communication.

4D Key Point

Be assertive on both the substance and the relationship.

In their second meeting, Kerry reiterates the goal of clearer communication and also candidly describes the team's financial situation. He explains that he felt Monique was accusing the team of withholding money. Their discussion goes well.

The substance goal of Monique and Kerry's third meeting is to discuss Helen's compensation and perks. Before their meeting, Monique sets trust as her relationship goal. She remembers to be as straightforward as possible without hurting her client's interests.

MEETING	RELATIONSHIP GOAL
First	Collegiality, mutual respect
Second	Clear communication
Third	Trust

DEALING WITH MULTI-ISSUE NEGOTIATIONS

A principle I strongly recommend adopting—especially in complex multi-issue negotiations—is to reach an understanding on how agreements will be made. Adopting a tentative agreement approach is very helpful here. Think tentative agreements contingent on the whole, meaning that when you make agreements on specific issues, this agreement is not finalized until all issues are settled. Whether the agreement becomes final depends on what happens with the whole agreement—whether it still makes sense when the big picture is considered in the end. Tentative agreements are discussed in more detail in Chapter 7—Step 4. Decide: Close the Negotiation.

Step 2: Construct an Agenda

Carefully constructing your agenda will allow you to use the ICON model to its fullest advantage. It will help you focus issue by issue on the interests, options, and criteria you need to know to make a wise decision in the end. Jointly prepare your negotiation agenda as far ahead of your first session as possible. In complex multi-issue negotiations, consider how you will order the issues. Beginning with big-picture issues (like deciding on the goal for your alliance) often makes it easier to resolve detailed or harder issues later on by providing the framework or philosophy for

---

Tactic Alert

Another Bite of the Apple

This tactic occurs when you are negotiating issue by issue and the other negotiator reopens discussions on a "closed" issue. There are legitimate reasons for reopening issues, but sometimes this action is a difficult tactic. Use the tentative agreement approach and jointly decide ahead of time that if someone wants to reopen an issue, he or she will need to make a persuasive argument for doing so. Spend time understanding why the issue is being reopened. Understand the other party's interests. Share yours, as well as your constraints. Agree that if changed circumstances are the cause of reopening, verification will be required as needed.

Tactic Alert

Cherry-Picking

This tactic occurs when you are negotiating issue by issue and the other negotiator tries to maximize his or her "take" on each issue without regard to the whole agreement. Be clear during the Design step that you are making tentative agreements contingent on the whole to help prevent cherry-picking. Point out this behavior if you see it emerge so that you can keep the negotiation on track. Set this and your other expectations up front. Explain the links you see between key issues, and discuss these in relation to interests and criteria. Evaluate the agreement as a whole during your negotiation.

---

resolving subissues. It can also help build rapport and momentum and provide an initial flow to the dialogue. Resolving easier issues first also helps build trust. This doesn't mean that you should leave the most difficult issues until the end. The danger of doing so is that if the last issue on the agenda is a critical one, then a "no" means that the parties will walk away with no agreement; everyone would have been better off learning this earlier. Therefore, start with easier issues early on, but move to critical issues fairly quickly.

Sometimes it's helpful to get outside help when constructing an agenda, especially if the agreement—a labor agreement, for instance, or a diplomatic treaty—will affect people away from the negotiating table. In such cases it is worth asking how to consult or involve others; perhaps there are people who have expertise and can provide useful data. Consider the goals and determine whether other people are needed and at what level of involvement. This helps build stakeholder and constituent support and lessens the likelihood that they will block a deal later on.

Let's go to the Helen Hoops negotiation to see what an agenda for the second meeting looks like. The substance goal for this meeting is to define Helen's responsibilities with the team (the roles she might fill such as captain or player-coach), and the conditions of her contract (such as length, no trade clauses, and so on). The relationship goal of this meeting is clear communication. Here's what an agenda might look like:

Meeting Agenda for Hoops Negotiation

1. Summary/reflections on last meeting
2. Responsibilities
3. Conditions
4. Next steps
5. Agenda for next meeting

For the first agenda item, Monique plans to raise the issue of clear communication—specifically, to check with Kerry on their previous discussion regarding the team's financial situation. For the next two items, Monique and Kerry will go through interests, options, and appropriate criteria, and attempt to create tentative agreements.

CONSIDER GROUND RULES AND ROLES

Without first making an effort to properly design your negotiation, it can become chaotic, thus increasing your susceptibility to difficult tactics. One such difficult tactic negotiators use is to try to get you to commit early to their preferred outcome. They leave little or no room for exploring interests or thinking "outside the box." With such negotiators, anything you say is taken as an offer rather than as just an option to consider. You may find it difficult to keep the other negotiator from latching onto and not letting go of any suggested solution you might make. By setting the ground rule early that a specified amount of time will be spent brainstorming without evaluation or commitment, you can prevent this grabbing tactic from being used on you.

Labor and management teams that have been adversarial in the past often create communication ground rules for a negotiation in order to change the dynamic—rules that, for instance, allow only one person to speak at a time. Ultimately, the ground rules are not important in and of themselves, but they are important as a means of improving communication between the parties.

Another technique for improving communication is to assign roles, particularly if there are a number of team members involved in a negotiation. Having different individuals take notes, keep time, and facilitate a session helps increase efficiency. If there are multiple issues where different individuals have specific knowledge or expertise, it may be useful in the Design step to assign the lead to those individuals. Larger teams sometimes give the role of observer to an individual so that person can more dispassionately observe how negotiations are going and then provide insight. As you begin negotiations, sharing these roles or assigning roles jointly creates a more collaborative tone.

People Skills

Focus on the People: Put Aside the Negotiation

Remember throughout your negotiation that you should separate the people from the problem and balance your statements with questions. Given that the Design step is the beginning of your interaction, it is crucial to immediately model behavior you would like to see throughout the negotiation. Consider the following example:

Sales account manager Andy had a huge challenge with a certain customer. This customer consistently cancelled appointments—not a few days in advance, but after Andy had already arrived in the reception area after a two-hour drive. On the rare occasion that the appointment was honored, Andy wasn't able to get anything accomplished. Ideas were shot down as "not a priority." Six months of time and effort yielded nothing but frustration and paranoia.

Andy couldn't drop the customer—the company was too important to his company—but he had to find a way to understand the customer's behavior. In their next meeting, Andy asked the customer to focus entirely on their relationship and to help him better understand the customer's needs. For starters, Andy offered that he felt like he was wasting the customer's time. The customer agreed—he didn't think their relationship could develop because the priorities of Andy's company were "misaligned." Andy was perplexed by this perception, but now that he knew details of his customer's concerns, he had an opportunity to delve into them. As it turned out, his customer's perceptions were based on third-hand information and weren't accurate. His customer also felt mistreated by the company's previous account managers and was unsettled by the fact that they were constantly changing. Andy was relieved by this candid conversation and his customer was grateful.

Andy hadn't tried to sell his customer or talk about his company's products. The conversation itself was critical. In one day, Andy reversed a three-year history of ineffectiveness—of account managers being unable to do anything with this account. The customer was delighted as well. "No one from your company has ever taken the time to understand my concerns," he commented. A productive, positive working relationship developed from that point and yielded business for Andy's company and satisfied his customer.

Be aware of an emotional wall. If the other party is experiencing strong emotions, they may not be able to hear anything you say. You may need to stop focusing on substance and deal directly with the people issue. In negotiations, people are at the table, too—not just "substance." They can be upset, angry, or frustrated. In these situations, talking about substance can be like talking to a wall. Focus instead on active listening and empathy.

4D Key Point

When emotions run high, stop focusing on the problem and start focusing on the people.

4D Key Point

When team negotiating, provide specific roles to individuals.

Step 3: Deliver A Core Message

Before beginning negotiations, consider your main message. Look to your substance and relationship goals and then craft a core message to deliver through your words and even your body language. Maybe the core message is, "We would bring lots of value as a partner to your company." Maybe the core message is, "I am a person who will work well with you over the long term." Politicians or people interviewed by the media are told to stay "on message" because they have a goal they are trying to achieve. Of course, when this is poorly done it seems phony and artificial. When it's done naturally and with integrity, it's leadership, persuasion, and courage.

You are framing the negotiation and telling a story. Negotiation is about persuading and influencing your counterparts. Like a lawyer delivering opening arguments to a jury or a narrator introducing characters in a novel, the person appeals to you to suspend disbelief and show willingness to entertain a viewpoint. Whether you are attempting to expand or cut the pie in negotiation, framing your story at the very beginning is crucial to your success.

A good core message will help keep you on track in your negotiations. Remember to focus on the impact on the other parties and not just on the intent of your message. A well-delivered core message should be the main impression your negotiation counterpart keeps as she or he walks away from the negotiation.

KNOW YOUR OPENING LINE

It's often said that first impressions are lasting ones. Know your opening lines to get the negotiation going in the right direction and to begin hitting the core message. Let's say that the core message is, "Create joint value." An opening line might be: "We're excited to be talking about a partnership here. I truly believe that we have the opportunity to create an agreement that will serve us both extremely well. We are ready to spend today listening to your goals and vision because we think that will ultimately help us create something with the most value."

As you prepare, I suggest you write down your opening line and say it aloud. How does it sound to you? To your team members? Although you may not say the same words when the negotiation begins, you can be proactive in your efforts to expand the pie right from the beginning. Know that your opening line points toward your core message, which in turn supports your substance and relationship goals. The impression you make with your opening line should support what you want to accomplish in your negotiation.

In the Helen Hoops negotiation, each party focuses on the main message it wants to send. Kerry wants Monique to walk away from their first negotiation meeting with the impression that, "The Golden Gaters will do their best to create a win-win agreement with Helen Hoops." Kerry wants to send this message because the Gaters want Helen as a part of a team that will contend for the championship.

Monique's core message is, "The Golden Gaters are Helen's first choice. All Helen asks is that any offer you make be on par with other offers." Monique wants the Gaters to be aware that Helen would prefer to stay with them but that she is looking at other teams and they should not be offended by this.

SMART NEGOTIATOR TIP

Tell a Vivid Story

Negotiation is ultimately about persuasion. You can alter the value placed on an issue by sharing a powerful story. If the information is more available to a person, that person will rely on it to make a negotiation decision. Well-told stories stick in our brains and persuade us more than reams of data.

One study provided two groups of participants acting as jurors with different closing arguments for a trial involving contract claims between a subcontractor and a contractor. In one closing argument, the contractor's claim had 10 vivid statements, while the other closing argument presented 10 dull statements. One vivid statement example was, "The slab was jagged and had to be sanded." In the dull version, this line was replaced with, "The slab was rough and had to be planed." With the vivid arguments, the contractor won 82 percent of the time versus 46 percent with the dull arguments.

Imagine that your kitchen sink has sprung a leak. Telling your landlord that water is spraying out and covering the floors is much more likely to be quickly resolved than simply saying that the faucet is leaking. When you are framing the negotiation, select distinct words and tell memorable stories.

CONCLUSION

In the Design step, consider the complexity of your negotiation and the time you will need to deal with it properly. If you're kicking off a complex negotiation, perhaps all you'll do in the first meeting is share and prioritize interests. If it's a simple negotiation, you may go through all the 4D steps in a single meeting. Figuring out what to expect is a necessary first step to shaping the goals and agenda of your negotiation. If you do your design job well, you will set up the other phases of your negotiation for success.

SUMMARY AND DESIGN CHECKLIST

Use the following questions to help you plan your Design step:

1. Set goals
   a. What is your substance goal for this meeting to move the negotiation forward?
   b. What is your relationship goal with the negotiation parties?
2. Construct an agenda
   a. Given the goal and the tangible document you want to create from that goal, what should be in the agenda? Consider the ICON negotiation framework.
   b. Do you need ground rules? Which ones?
   c. Who should be at the meeting? Will it be helpful for people to have roles like facilitator, timekeeper, and note-taker?
3. Deliver a core message
   a. What is the core message you are trying to deliver via what you say and how you act?

Review the following example from the Helen Hoops negotiation—the Design Checklist for Helen's agent Monique.

Design Checklist for Helen's Agent

1. Set goals

a) **Substance:** Joint proposal on responsibilities and conditions

b) **Relationship:** Collegiality, mutual respect

2. Construct an agenda

a) **Agenda:**
   1. Summary/reflections on last meeting
   2. Responsibilities (interests, options)
   3. Conditions (interests, options)
   4. Next steps
   5. Agenda for next meeting

b) **Ground rules:** Brainstorm first before evaluating.

c) **Roles:** Monique and Kerry will lead the meeting. Coach will come to provide expertise on different team responsibilities Helen might assume.

3. Deliver a core message

a) **Kerry's core message:** "Golden Gaters will do their best to create a win-win agreement with Helen Hoops."

b) **Monique's core message:** "Golden Gaters are Helen's first choice. All Helen asks is that any offer be on par with other offers."

QuickGuide: The Design Phase

Definition	In the Design step, you set up and begin the negotiation process.
Importance	Proper design sets the stage for a win-win approach to negotiating, making it easier to discuss interests, options, and criteria, and to expand the pie. It also helps parties avoid win-lose negotiating.
Preparation	Prepare your goals, both on substance and relationship. Draft a possible agenda to meet those goals. Figure out your core message.
Dialogue	Question: "Let's discuss what we really want to accomplish today. What are our goals for this meeting?"
	Statement: "It's critical from my perspective to decide this issue today, because of our external deadlines."
Tips	Jointly confirm goals, both on substance and relationship. Jointly create an agenda to meet these goals. Remember your core message.

YOUR NEGOTIATION WORKSHEET

Now return to your negotiation. Write your answers to the Design summary questions on the worksheet that follows.

Your Negotiation Worksheet

Design Checklist

Set Goals

    a)   Substance:

    b)   Relationship:

Construct an Agenda

    a)   Agenda:

    b)   Ground rules:

    c)   Roles:

Deliver a Core Message

    a)   Core message:

REVIEW (*SEE ANSWER KEY AT END OF CHAPTER*)

Check all that apply

1. What benefits should you expect from designing your negotiations well?
   __ a) Prevent haggling
   __ b) Keep the other party from asking questions
   __ c) Provide a path to crush the other side
   __ d) Improve the working relationship in your negotiation

2. The basic elements of effective negotiation design include:
   __ a) Constructing an agenda
   __ b) Sharing mutual options up front
   __ c) Setting goals
   __ d) Getting the other party to make the first offer
   __ e) Delivering a core message

3. What are examples of relationship goals?
   __ a) Increased trust
   __ b) A contract agreement
   __ c) Collegial and friendly relationship
   __ d) Getting tentative agreements on each issue
   __ e) Respect

True or False

   __ 1. Look to the relationship goal(s) to craft a core message.
   __ 2. It's not useful to assign specific roles to individuals in a negotiation.
   __ 3. Dealing with the relationship may be helpful when emotions run high.
   __ 4. Starting with easier issues might prevent the building of trust and momentum.
   __ 5. Focusing on the Design step decreases your susceptibility to difficult tactics.

ANSWER KEY

Check all that apply

1. What benefits should you expect from designing your negotiations well?
    a) Yes. A main purpose of jointly discussing your negotiation process is to keep the parties from getting caught up in haggling.
    b) No. While effective design may help prevent difficult tactics, it does not prevent questions. Effective design encourages questions throughout the negotiation. The more collaborative the process, the more likely effective questions are being asked, such as "Does this draft agenda meet your needs?" or, "Should we bring in an expert on that topic?"
    c) No. This approach does not set you up to destroy the other party.
    d) Yes. Developing positive relationships is a key aspect of effective negotiation design.

2. The basic elements of effective negotiation design include:
    a) Yes. Constructing an agenda is critical to organizing the interaction.
    b) No. While it is certainly helpful to eventually share options that meet both parties' interests, this is usually not the best place to start.
    c) Yes. Parties should set both substance and relationship goals beforehand.
    d) No. Getting the other party to make the first offer may lead to haggling. At some later point it may be fine that the other party starts generating options, but doing so right away may be more harmful than helpful.
    e) Yes. Delivering a core message helps keep the negotiation focused.

3. What are examples of relationship goals?
   a) Yes. Increased trust is an example of a preferred working relationship between the parties.
   b) No. A contract agreement is an example of a substance goal.
   c) Yes. Collegial and friendly are qualities that describe how the parties might relate to each other.
   d) No. Getting tentative agreements on each issue is an approach to negotiating, not a relationship goal. Getting tentative agreements does help improve the relationship because both parties understand and agree on how to come to agreement.
   e) Yes. Respect may be an important relationship goal that is independent of whether or not the parties come to an agreement.

True or False

1. True. Relationship goals are often closely related to a core message. Look to substance goals as well.
2. False. It is useful to assign specific roles to individuals in a negotiation. Assigning roles like facilitator, note-taker, and timekeeper can help increase the efficiency and quality of a negotiation.
3. True. Dealing with the relationship and setting aside the substance may be very helpful when emotions run high because there may be an emotional wall put up by the other party, making that party unable to hear anything on the topics being negotiated.
4. False. Starting with easier issues helps build trust and momentum by getting smaller agreements, thus providing optimism and common ground.
5. True. Focusing on the Design step decreases your susceptibility to difficult tactics because you are clear on your goals and can be more proactive and cooperative in your efforts to reach those goals.

6

Steps 2 and 3. Dig for Interests and Develop Options

The 4D Dig and Develop steps

are where you "dig" for value in your negotiation and "develop"—brainstorm and evaluate—your choices.

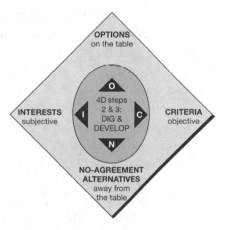

THE CHALLENGE

In California, drinking water is a precious commodity, often in short supply. Residents of San Francisco and the surrounding area obtain most of their drinking water from a distant mountain dam built on a major river. Other rural and farming communities also draw water from this river, including several large agricultural water districts. Because of the reduced water flows resulting from so many groups drawing water from the river, the fish habitat began deteriorating and the federal government, at the urging of environmental groups, directed all the entities to reduce the amount of water they pumped from the river.

San Francisco argued that its share should not be reduced because doing so would cause major economic harm to the region and because other affordable water sources were unavailable. The agricultural districts, although able to reduce their water draw without significant impact, balked at giving up any water because this surplus served as a cushion during droughts. Further, the agricultural districts felt that giving up water would set an unwanted precedent and could harm their state water rights. All parties were ready to go to court to fight any reduction.

THE SOLUTION

By digging at underlying interests and developing "expand-the-pie" options, a creative deal was fashioned. San Francisco had few affordable water resource alternatives, but it did have financial strength. The agricultural districts needed additional funds to finance their growth, but had water to spare. As a solution, San Francisco entered into long-term contracts to pay agricultural districts to decrease their water draw by an amount equal to San Francisco's required reduction. This solution included a provision that, in the event of a drought, agricultural districts would be released from their contract requirements and have their original share restored.

This innovative agreement allowed San Francisco to maintain its water draw from the river, thus protecting its economy. San Francisco also avoided having to buy high-priced water from alternative sources. Agricultural districts received needed funds by selling their surplus water and were protected from future droughts. Because less water overall was being drawn from the river, the fish habitat improved, and environmental groups and the federal government were satisfied.

SOURCE: TIM DAYONOT

The Dig and Develop steps of the negotiation process put the ICON Value Diamond to work. Getting interests on the table is the first step, followed by generating options and then filtering these through criteria. The Dig and Develop steps are crucial for creating value. Too often, negotiators jump directly to the Decide step and begin haggling, conceding, com-

> ## Overview: DIG and DEVELOP
>
> ### Focusing on Dig and Develop
>
> - Gets ICON elements on the table
> - Is crucial for creating value (digging)
> - Is crucial for narrowing and evaluating choices (developing)
>
> ## Bottom Line
>
> Dig and Develop are the main steps in which to use ICON to expand the pie.

promising, and bartering—they begin cutting the pie before expanding it. If you've done an effective job in the Design step, you will have jointly carved out time to focus on sharing interests and preempted the urge to leap too quickly to final decision making.

I call these second and third steps of the negotiation process "Dig" and "Develop" to focus on the expansion of possibility (digging) and the choices that come from brainstorming and evaluating (developing). "Dig" represents the need to probe for interests and go beneath positions as obvious solutions. "Develop" represents the need to brainstorm and narrow possible options by filtering them through criteria.

In effect, digging and developing are two sides of the same coin. While they are separate activities, they are really linked together. The reality of negotiating is that you often go issue by issue, not task by task. That is, parties often dig and develop one issue before moving to the next. They don't necessarily focus on all interests first, then all options, then all criteria—the real-life back-and-forth dynamic is less rigid. Indeed, parties often forget to really dig at all—to probe for interests, brainstorm options, and explicitly discuss criteria. Negotiations become restricted and narrow when parties just make offers and counteroffers. Digging and developing are both important, and the explicit separation we emphasize between the two should help you remember to do both.

4D Key Point

Negotiating is an interactive activity, so you won't always do everything in a strict order.

Most of your dig and develop time should be spent inside the ICO triangle—in the upper half of the ICON Value Diamond. You can stay inside the triangle and build a solution by connecting interests, options, and criteria.

However, over the years I have also seen effective negotiators make a conscious choice of *collaboratively* bringing no-agreement alternatives or BATNAs into the conversation to enhance problem solving. Bringing no-agreement alternatives to the table provides instant information on primary interests that are driving the negotiation; these alternatives can also be effectively used as criteria. Alternatives at the table can also help accelerate a negotiation, in either direction—toward a point where both parties feel an agreement is fair, or toward a point where they conclude that no agreement should be reached.

4D Key Point

Discussing no-agreement alternatives is a critical tool of win-win negotiating.

Be aware that the choice to put a BATNA on the table must be handled with the highest degree of caution and sensitivity. Telling a party you are considering working with someone else can have a huge emotional impact on the other party. In many situations I would recommend not putting your BATNA on the table. Perhaps raising it will send the other side to its BATNA, at which point both parties might feel compelled to just skip ahead to "decide" strategies. Perhaps the other party will just be offended that you felt it necessary to threaten instead of negotiate.

So how do you actually dig and develop in a negotiation setting? The rest of this chapter is devoted to this matter. Because negotiation cannot be scripted, having ICON as a map of the negotiation allows you to go back and forth between the four elements.

Step 1: Dig for Interests

You must probe for the underlying interests of the other party to truly understand the other sides' needs. Reveal your own interests to help the other person recognize what you really care about.

ASK QUESTIONS TO DIG FOR OTHER PARTY'S INTERESTS

I mentioned earlier that most negotiators don't spend enough time asking questions, or that they don't ask the *right* questions. For various reasons, we often think—incorrectly so—that great negotiators are people who have all the answers and that bold sound bites are more powerful than probing questions.

Asking questions shows curiosity, interest, and concern. It reduces misperceptions and mistaken assumptions. Furthermore, the only way value is really created—the only way the pie is expanded—is by probing. Under the old us-them paradigm, negotiations are about knowing everything, not showing weakness, and not asking questions. A cardinal mistake that many of these old-style negotiators repeat time and again is to make many arguments and statements and ask few questions. Questions asked are often rhetorical or leading. Such negotiators also tend not to be good listeners, and being able to listen well is a critical skill for achieving collaborative, successful, larger-pie outcomes.

How do you focus on the right questions to ask if you don't have much information going in? Start with *general* open-ended questions regarding needs, concerns, and desires. Follow these up with more *specific* questions to show that you're listening and moving the dialogue forward. Then, articulate *reflective* or active listening questions to create confirmation of understanding. The box on the next page contains examples of this focused question strategy.

Another approach is to take a more direct value questioning strategy (not "value" as in morals and principles, of course). At a basic level,

4D Focused Question Examples

General questions

- What's important to you in this matter?
- What's the big picture for you here?

Specific questions

- Within that issue, what are the key concerns?
- Can you tell me more about your manager's need for confidentiality?

Reflective questions

- Being treated fairly and being compensated for your financial losses are the interests that I have heard so far. Would it be right to infer that you have felt unfairly dealt with up to now?
- Given what you just said about the deadline, do you think we share an interest in getting this done sooner rather than later?

negotiation is about trying to enhance satisfaction and happiness. Asking questions that make the value on the table explicit enhances the possibility of getting a better agreement (or sometimes, getting any agreement at all).

Start with challenge questions. Focus on the problems and opportunities the other party faces in the negotiation. Understanding these will provide insight into what value can be created at the table. Then go to consequence questions on the negatives and positives that might occur as the result of a challenge. By doing so, you draw out critical needs to craft the best possible value-added solution.

Challenge and consequence questions will help you deal with the other party's positions because the responses to these questions will help you—and maybe even the other party—discover underlying interests. These questions also help make implicit interests explicit, which will help when brainstorming options. The skill practice box on the next page provides an example of the value question strategy.

When you face position or demand statements in a negotiation, use this as a cue to ask questions about underlying interests. Rather than getting frustrated, reframe. Test what you think is the interest. Better yet, ask

Examples of 4D Value Questions

Challenge Questions

- Can you describe your dissatisfaction with your computer service system?
- What don't you like about the house you currently live in?
- What are the challenges you face with regard to your current book-keeping practices?

Consequence Questions

- What are the consequences of your computers going offline twice a week?
- Since you don't have a backyard, what do your kids do for recreation?
- If your bookkeeping speed improved by 25 percent, how would your organization benefit?

Skill Practice

Asking Interest Questions When Faced with Positions

Read the stated position and guess the party's possible interests. Consider questions you might ask to discover those interests.

Other Party's Stated Position

- I won't agree unless you make it a guaranteed three-year contract.

Other Party's Possible Interests

- Wants to win
- Wants to be treated equitably (they heard another company received a three-year contract)
- Wants stability
- Wants financials to be consistent

Interest Questions You Might Ask

- Why three years? (a specific question)
- Can you tell me why less than three years won't work? (a challenge question)
- How does a longer number of years provide value to you? (a consequences question)

4D Key Point

Respond to position or demand statements with interest questions.

---

for the underlying need for the statement you just heard. Ask, "Why?" or, "What will that help you achieve?"

When a client makes a position statement about how much she is willing to pay you, some of her possible underlying interests might be to stay within budget, set a precedent for the payment of other consultants, or look good to her manager. Examples of interest questions you might ask include, "Do you have any concerns that I am unaware of?" or "Are there budgetary issues?" Instead of going right to a counteroffer, ask questions to uncover creative solutions, gain time to reflect, and protect you from pressure to give in. Estimating ahead of time what some of the other party's interests might be helps you craft better interest questions.

When a child blurts out a position statement such as, "I'm not going to sleep now!" her interest might simply be that she does not feel tired. However the child's interests might also be to test her parents' limits, to watch the end of a movie, or be treated like her friends who stay up late. It's important to find out, because the option you select will depend on which interest or interests are behind the position. The interest question for this situation might be, "Why are you asking to stay up later?"

Think of your own negotiations where the other side has made a position statement. Remember that positions are just options about which the other party has become rigid or inflexible. Try to come up with at least three interests of the person with whom you are negotiating. Then come up with three interest questions. Write your answers in the negotiation worksheet on the next page.

SHARE YOUR INTERESTS

Whether or not the other party asks for your interests, it's still important to share them. In order to be as constructive as possible, remember that your interests are different from your positions. Positions are inflexible demands for specific options; interests are deeper—your underlying motivations.

Negotiation Worksheet

Digging for Interests

Their Position _____

_____

_____

_____

_____

Their Possible Interests _____

_____

_____

_____

_____

_____

_____

_____

Your Interests Questions _____

_____

_____

_____

_____

_____

_____

_____

People Skills

Dealing with Win-Lose Adversarial Negotiators: A Fundamental Issue of Approach

It's much easier to have win-win negotiating when parties trust each other and have a history. You will occasionally encounter negotiators who are positional and adversarial, though. Take this into account in your negotiating strategy, but don't necessarily change your style. For example, you may need to not disclose facts that make you vulnerable. Regardless of how the other party acts, it's rarely useful to mirror "difficult" tactics. This often deteriorates into attrition and negativity. From a negotiation design point of view, take your concerns into account in your core message. Perhaps it's, "I'm committed to a negotiation that provides value to all parties. I won't accept any other approach from anyone here today, and I promise to do my best to not be negatively influenced by any other approach." Then act accordingly. Staying focused on a positive core message will win over more people than you might think. In later phases of the negotiation, knowing the type of negotiator you are dealing with will help shape your decision regarding what to disclose, what to offer, and how to arrive at a final agreement.

It's important not to demonize the people we perceive to be difficult negotiators (though venting for a while can sometimes help). Understanding the other person's behavior—not to be confused with excusing it—can ultimately create an approach that is comfortable for all parties. Maybe they don't trust your organization. Maybe someone has cheated them in past negotiations. Maybe they simply don't know another way to negotiate. In the end, we are all advocates of our own self-interests, and each of us believes what we are doing will produce the best outcome. Understanding this and helping the other party understand your goals and strategy will lead all the parties toward something better.

4D Key Point

You can use an expand-the-pie approach regardless of what the other side does.

Step 2: Develop Options

There are two important behaviors to keep in mind when developing options. First, separate inventing from deciding. Second, invite and share options.

SEPARATE INVENTING FROM DECIDING

Good negotiators create a comfortable atmosphere for discussing options. This is a core issue when it comes to brainstorming. Freewheeling option generation can lead to creative solutions that can be arrived at in no other way. However, some people are so used to positional concession-based negotiating that it can very difficult to brainstorm. They will latch onto any idea that might suit them, or they are unwilling to create new options for fear of commitment. Be clear with each other that all ideas will be put on the table without commitment—that you will create value by investigating many possibilities.

Another impediment to brainstorming is the fact that many people are more comfortable critiquing ideas than coming up with them—many people are more accustomed to trying to find the one "right" answer from a list of choices. Articulate that the goal is to get ideas out there; evaluating will come later.

Take care that brainstormed options aren't anchored in specific numbers and terms—it's better to come up with concepts at this time. Anchoring is an attempt—albeit not necessarily a deliberate or malicious one—to influence the negotiation to a range more favorable to one party. While it's helpful to let the other party know your range, it's too early to debate specific numbers, which may come across as positions.

Tactic Alert

Hoarding

Hoarding happens when a negotiator latches onto any idea you put out there. This dynamic makes it difficult for you to discuss a range of ideas and proposals. Before you negotiate, agree that the two of you are brainstorming—that you are inventing options at this stage, not deciding. If the other party starts to latch onto ideas, remind him or her that you are not offering these ideas for commitment.

4D Key Point

Effective negotiators don't just listen to words; they listen for what the other side really cares about.

INVITE AND SHARE OPTIONS

Ask the other party to share options. When dealing with those who are less spontaneous at the table, ask them to brainstorm beforehand. Share your options with the other party, especially options that truly meet their interests. Provide different formulas or perspectives that help the person see that you truly want to explore different ideas.

The following are sample questions to break the ice when it is time to explore options:

Sample Questions to Explore Options

- "What are three ways we could satisfy this interest in improving communication among employees?"
- "Here's two ways we could do it. Do you have other possible solutions?"
- "Does anyone have any ideas, no matter how crazy, to start us off on how to meet our deadline? Just throw something out—it doesn't have to be carefully thought out."

As options emerge, you may discover more interests. This provides you with the opportunity to check the interests you hear and make them explicit. This can lead to greater creativity as you brainstorm further options.

Consider the option-sharing statements on the next page and the possible interests they reveal. Note in these statements that using words like "could" or "one idea" or "one option" conveys that there are many possibilities.

DETERMINE WHICH OPTIONS BEST MEET THE INTERESTS

Compare your list of options to your list of interests. Look particularly for options that meet your shared, prioritized interests. If one option bubbles up as the best, that's great, but resist the temptation to prematurely decide on one rather than moving more options through the filtering process. This is often where "crazy" options are looked at more carefully and may lead to a different option, but one that just might work.

OPTION STATEMENT	POSSIBLE INTEREST
• "One option is to outsource the project, another option is to do it in-house, and a third is to somehow divide the work between in-house and outsourcing."	• Finishing work on time
• "We could have the meeting in Hawaii and our expenses would be tax deductible."	• Having a good time, having a meeting, and being fiscally responsible
• "One idea is to go to the early movie and then have dinner."	• Spending more time together
• "We could paint the house ourselves and use the money we save to get new carpet."	• Sprucing the house up and being financially savvy
• "We could vote on it."	• Fairness, majority satisfaction, movement toward closure

USE CRITERIA TO TEST THE RANGE OF POSSIBILITIES

No one wants to be taken advantage of in a negotiation. Indeed, most people need to explain to someone—their manager, their colleague, or themselves—why an agreement is fair. During the Develop phase of a negotiation, the goal is to narrow down the realm of possibility to what's doable and agreeable. Apply criteria to your brainstormed options so you can weed out the less desirable ones and select others for further exploration.

Skills Practice

Asking Effective Criteria Questions

As you discuss criteria, you may fall into the trap of becoming positional and adversarial—focusing on the criterion you think is absolutely right can be as positional as focusing on the interest or option you think is right. The outcome can be deadlock. Suppose, for instance, you are trying to sell your car. You might continually point to the criterion that favors you—let's say the Blue Book price—even though the local market price is lower because of a glut of similar cars. If you and the other party can agree on criteria, that's good, but if you can't, that's fine too. What's important is to understand the rationale the other person is expressing. That's why asking questions at this stage can be as important as in the interests and options phases. Here are a few examples of criteria questions:

- "What criteria did you look at when you came up with that number?"
- "Do you know how we might access the industry standards here?"
- "Are there outside experts who could provide a neutral perspective on this situation?"
- "Do you have any information on agreements your colleagues have made?"
- "What does the contract say?"
- "What do other associates in this firm with four years of experience make?"
- "What was the protocol for your predecessor?"

Write down other effective criteria questions.

_____

_____

_____

No one wants to waste time, either—to spend a long time negotiating and discover only near the end of the process that you were miles apart all along. Apply your criteria for what constitutes an acceptable range of outcomes to help predict whether an agreement is even worth pursuing.

Skills Practice

Making Effective Criteria Statements

Your ability to make criteria statements without being perceived as adversarial is also important. In the criteria discussion, a joint problem-solving tone helps keep it positive and constructive. At the same time it's important to be an advocate and protect your own interests. Putting criteria on the table lets the other party know what you perceive as reasonable in this situation. Clearly, you don't want to create the perception that you're willing to accept less than what's fair and appropriate, especially when one of your primary interests is getting the best deal possible. Some possible criteria statements include:

- "Why don't we look on the Internet together to see the price range for this product."
- "When it comes to figuring out the amount of staff, budget, and resources for this project, I recommend we look at what this department did with similar projects over the last year."
- "I think more research to see what other companies have been doing will provide some useful comparison points."

Write down other effective criteria statements.

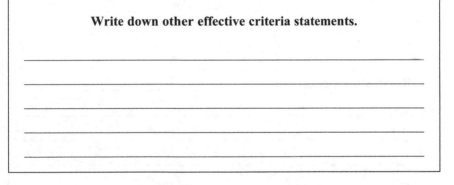

You can also cut off negotiation early if you have had quality conversations regarding interests and options and just can't see where it would be beneficial for the parties to enter into an agreement.

On the worksheet on the following page, apply these techniques to your own negotiation.

ENHANCE AND ADJUST THE BEST FEW OPTIONS

To make the next phase—Decide—worthwhile, your list of options should be viable. They may have to be better understood, developed a

Your Negotiation Worksheet

Developing Options

Criteria Questions to Ask _____

_____

_____

_____

_____

_____

_____

_____

_____

_____

_____

Criteria Statements _____

_____

_____

_____

_____

_____

_____

_____

_____

4D Key Point

Be assertive with interests and flexible with options.

---

bit more, or researched, but they should have potential. As you start narrowing your list, remember you're still an advocate for your interests. A win-win approach doesn't require giving in, especially on your primary interests. At the same time, being flexible with how you meet interests allows for creative problem solving.

BE READY TO DEAL WITH NO-AGREEMENT ALTERNATIVES

No-agreement alternatives are arguably the most difficult thing to deal with at the negotiating table. Raising a no-agreement alternative is often perceived as a threat. "Take it or leave it" is one such negotiation threat. Yet collaborative negotiators can bring no-agreement alternatives to the table to *enhance* the ability of parties to work together.

Consider Sylvia, a chief financial officer, who is trying to find a new accounting firm for her company. In a meeting with Jerry, a partner in Accounting Firm A, Sylvia mentions that her company is also looking at Accounting Firm B.

"You know," she says, "Accounting Firm B has submitted a proposal to us, and their rates are about 15 percent lower than what you have quoted."

Aware that he doesn't want to appear defensive, Jerry acknowledges, "I'm sure their rates are lower. However, throughout our 75-year history we have determined that our slightly higher rates are necessary to maintain the attention, accuracy, and satisfaction our clients want."

"Can you justify that in this case?" Sylvia asks.

"It's not in either of our best interests if we can't bring all of our competencies to bear," Jerry replies. "We could be sued, and you could go bankrupt if we are not attentive and accurate."

"Yes," says Sylvia, "but you don't want me to get these services elsewhere, do you?"

"I'd like to work with you," replies Jerry. "Believe me I would. However, if you choose to spend less, I will understand. I still hope you will see the value of our thoroughness sometime in the future."

Jerry did his ICON preparation before this meeting: He developed his BATNA and estimated Sylvia's as well. This is the key to having this conversation. Sylvia informed Jerry that his firm's prices are too high; Jerry cautioned Sylvia not to shop for accounting firms on the basis of price. Having made these interests clear to each other, they may be able to explore each interest in more depth and find mutually beneficial options.

SHOULD YOU DISCLOSE YOUR BATNA?

The decision of whether to disclose your BATNA is a crucial one that should not be taken lightly. Ask yourself first and foremost what you are trying to accomplish. Perhaps you want to have a deeper discussion, end a negotiation, speed it up, or test whether it's worth spending more time at the table. Disclosing your BATNA can also help create a better discussion and more options, and it can serve as a persuasive criterion.

Consider a salary negotiation. If your manager knows you have a job offer for considerably more than your current salary, it is often more persuasive than considering a raise based on factors such as your performance, the rate of inflation, or what people at similar jobs make, since there is a possibility of your leaving.

Tactic Alert

Chicken Little

We see it in the news every day: Party X says the sky is falling, and Party Y says it's fine. Both sides amass an impressive array of "facts," yet neither is listening. Debate rather than true dialogue is taking place. How can the wheat be separated from the chaff? Not easily, and sometimes not at all if facts are bent with the intent of supporting interests. Just as you can be positional with options, you can be positional with criteria. Seek to understand criteria without necessarily agreeing. Return to interests to probe more deeply.

Sharing your BATNA can be a demonstration of assertiveness. If the other party has a perception that you need the agreement badly and tries to take advantage of that, then providing your BATNA signals that you have no intention of signing a bad agreement.

Aside from these strategic considerations, some people prefer to disclose their BATNA to be straightforward and frank. When people begin to feel like the other parties are dancing around issues, it can reduce rapport and decrease trust. If you already have trust in your negotiating relationship or are trying to build it, it can be a good idea to reveal your BATNA because you're trying to get right to the point. This may help the negotiation, particularly from an efficiency perspective.

Be aware of your BATNA tipping point, and the other party's as well. Many of us reveal our BATNA when we've become fed up, angry, or frustrated. Before you reach this point, test yourself as to the consequences. Sleep on it or talk it through with a colleague or friends. Ask yourself whether you're trying to meet your own interests or simply trying to hurt the other party. If you see the other party getting close to his or her tipping point, consider changing the dynamic. Take a break, end the meeting, or go back to discussing interests you have in common.

What are the factors to consider in disclosure? Once your goal is clear, you still have to take into account a number of factors before deciding whether or not to disclose your BATNA. Examine the ramifications disclosure will have on the negotiation itself and on the other party. Given these, will you be able to accomplish your goal, or will it get sidetracked? Sometimes, no matter how artfully you state your BATNA, sharing it is a declaration of war, so consider a worst-case scenario and know your ability to walk.

How Should You Disclose Your BATNA?

Suppose you decide to disclose your BATNA. What next? How should you disclose it? This is the point where your communication and relationship-building skills come into play. You know your goal and have evaluated the impact of revealing your BATNA on the other party. Now consider how to minimize the negative consequences of sharing this information. In many situations, these consequences can't be prevented altogether: it's like telling someone you're dating that you're no longer interested. For the most part, there's nothing you can say or do that will make this conversation go smoothly. Acknowledging this will make it easier for you to disclose your BATNA.

Having said this, you can reduce the impact of disclosure by being transparent—by explaining the reason for putting your BATNA on the table (it may be helpful to explain what is not your reason—for example, you aren't trying to sound threatening). Transparency is important because when you're trying to communicate a stressful message and aren't completely forthcoming with your information, your listener is less likely to give you the benefit of the doubt. You're trying to focus on interests, not hurt the other party, so get all the information out there so both parties can make wise decisions.

Sharing your BATNA can come off as a threat, and you have to be able to defuse it. To do that, you have to be able to affirm your relationship, before, during, and after disclosure.

While these ideas can be called "techniques," keep in mind that they are intended as tools to help you unveil your motivations and desires, not to manipulate others or be deceitful.

ASKING ABOUT THE OTHER PARTY'S BATNA

Asking the other party to disclose his BATNA can help you understand his interests, provide criteria, create options, and create straightforward, frank conversation—the more you know, the better equipped you'll be to deal with it. Asking may also help the other party because he may be reluctant to disclose his BATNA unilaterally. Should you ask? Make this decision using the same thinking you use to decide whether to disclose your own BATNA. Be aware of situations where parties will be uncomfortable discussing alternatives. Some may not want to because of confidentiality concerns. Others who are more adversarial may not share information unless it provides an advantage to them.

How should you ask? Here are a few thoughts to make it easier:

- Acknowledge that not agreeing is a reality of negotiating.
- Affirm that we all have to do what's right for ourselves and our organizations.

4D Key Point

Walk directly to the BATNA instead of being defensive.

- Give the other party an out when you ask. Say, for instance, "To the extent that you're comfortable, can you share what your other possibilities are?"
- Articulate the goal of creating the best possible agreement. By understanding each other's BATNA, you may be able to generate a more creative offer. You can learn more about the other party's interests and ultimately meet those interests better if you understand her alternatives.

What happens when they tell you? Learn more about how the BATNA meets their needs. It doesn't make sense to bad-mouth the competition at this stage. Instead, acknowledge the BATNA's strengths; ask interest, challenge, and consequence questions; and offer an explanation of how you differentiate yourself from the BATNA. It is extremely powerful to be straightforward and honest in discussing their BATNA. It prevents you from looking defensive. If you don't think it's a big deal, they will see that. I call this technique "walking directly to the BATNA."

INFORMATION EXCHANGE

Negotiation involves the exchange of information. Much of this book involves ideas on how to gather information and how to provide it. Your ability to craft agreements that truly meet the interests of the parties is dependent on finding out and sharing useful information. Prior to and at the beginning of negotiation, finding out and sharing background information sets the stage for successful outcomes. Then throughout the rest of the negotiation, managing the information exchange means finding out facts that help parties collaborate or provide leverage for dividing the value. When you negotiate with others on the same team, group preparation on this topic gets the team on the same page and prevents problems and conflict.

A key issue in information exchange is disclosure. While I have already discussed disclosure of BATNA, disclosure on all the ICON elements must be contemplated. Carefully consider what and what not to disclose during the negotiation. Negotiators often hold their cards close to their vest, and this prevents the creation of value and increases distrust. However, people don't want to reveal information that makes them vulnerable to the other party. Consider the cost-benefit analysis. What is the benefit of sharing certain information? What's the harm?

In preparation for any negotiation use the three Gs of information exchange: Get, give, and guard. First, what information do you want to *get* or ask about? What facts of the situation do you want to know more about? As you do your ICON analysis, what more do you want to find out about the other party's interests? Using the type of questions described in this chapter will enable you to meet needs better. Remember that questions can propel a negotiation forward in ways that statements or arguments cannot.

Then, consider what information you want to *give* or share. The other side can often not meet your needs if it does not know what they are or if it does not know what is more important to you. What do you want to disclose factually that will move the negotiation forward? What do you want to disclose that will help the other side feel more comfortable? What information do you want to share that reveals your strength or firmness? For both the get and give categories, look directly to your ICON data to figure out your information exchange plan.

The last category to prepare for is whether to *guard* or protect information. Certain information may convey desperation or urgency, and revealing it will give the other side an unnecessary advantage. If I am negotiating to sell a vacation condominium to a potential buyer, I would guard the fact that I am in desperate need of money to pay off a personal debt.

YOUR INFORMATION EXCHANGE WORKSHEET

For an upcoming negotiation, fill out the following:

Get: (questions to ask)

Give: (information to disclose)

Guard: (information to protect)

CONCLUSION

Without a doubt, negotiation is about influence and persuasion. Because people view it this way, they forget it's often more powerful to spend time understanding rather than persuading. Understanding helps build the trust that makes communication clearer. As you dig in and develop your negotiation, think of yourself as a student trying to educate yourself about the other parties' interests, criteria, options, and no-agreement alternatives. The flip side of this is to try to understand your own ICON elements as well. You'll find understanding fruitful, if only because it is a precursor to everything else constructive in negotiation.

Better negotiators get more information and make more out of it. Whatever the substance aspects of your negotiation and whatever characteristics it might have, good negotiation skills help improve your relationship, and a strong working relationship elicits more information that generates better-fitting options. Discovering these options—expanding the pie in this way—will make your Decide step more efficient and help you create lasting agreements.

SMART NEGOTIATOR TIP

Find the Best Messenger

When you have a negative perception of someone, you are more likely to devalue ideas and options that the other party proposes. Imagine a husband and a wife getting a divorce. The wife suggests a way to divide up the assets. The husband, who is still nursing deep hurt, lashes out at her suggestion, even if it objectively meets his interests. However, if the suggestion had never been made by the wife and is instead supplied by the mediator, the proposal's merits are more likely to be disentangled from the hostility between the parties. Having a third party, such as a mutual friend or an expert in the field, suggest a solution makes it more palatable to the parties.

   This phenomenon is called *reactive devaluation*, and groundbreaking research on this concept was done by Lee Ross. He and others found reactive devaluation to occur even when a person was not trying to gain a negotiation advantage by devaluing the other side's proposal. This was important to focus on because there is a strategic benefit to flinching in an attempt to shift the other person's expectations.

SUMMARY AND DIG AND DEVELOP CHECKLIST

Use the following questions to help you plan your Dig and Develop steps.

DIG: Share and explore interests
DEVELOP: Brainstorm and evaluate options to make progress

1. Discover interests
   a) What questions will probe for the other party's interests (use strategies of general, specific, reflective, and value questions of challenge and consequence)?
   b) What interests do you want to share? What interests do you *not* want to disclose?
2. Brainstorm options
   a) What options might you try to draw out?
   b) What options do you want to put on the table? What options do you *not* want on the table?

3. Narrow through criteria
   a) What questions might you ask to find helpful criteria?
   b) What criteria statements will you provide? What criteria will you not provide?
4. Just in case, be ready to deal with no-agreement alternatives
   a) Will you disclose your BATNA?
   b) If you do disclose, how will you do it?
   c) Will you ask about the other party's BATNA, and if so, how?

Review the following example from the Helen Hoops negotiation—the Dig and Develop Checklist for Helen's agent Monique.

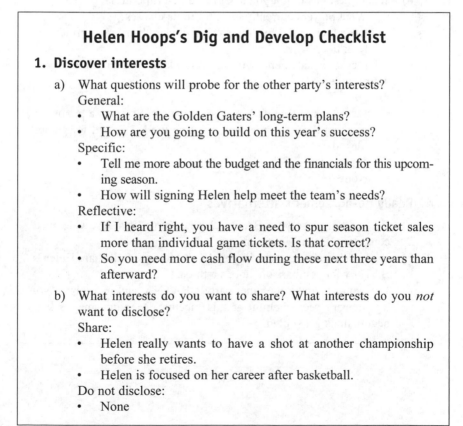

Helen Hoops's Dig and Develop Checklist

1. Discover interests

a) What questions will probe for the other party's interests?
General:
- What are the Golden Gaters' long-term plans?
- How are you going to build on this year's success?

Specific:
- Tell me more about the budget and the financials for this upcoming season.
- How will signing Helen help meet the team's needs?

Reflective:
- If I heard right, you have a need to spur season ticket sales more than individual game tickets. Is that correct?
- So you need more cash flow during these next three years than afterward?

b) What interests do you want to share? What interests do you *not* want to disclose?
Share:
- Helen really wants to have a shot at another championship before she retires.
- Helen is focused on her career after basketball.

Do not disclose:
- None

(continued on next page)

2. Brainstorm options

a) What options might you try to draw out?
   - Captain, player-coach, comp tickets

b) What options do you want to put on the table? What options do you *not* want on the table?
   On the table:
   - Multiple-year agreement, performance-based bonuses, no-trade clause

   Not on the table:
   - Hire Helen's dad as coach (Helen ultimately thinks this is not a good idea).

3. Narrow through criteria

a) What questions might you ask to find helpful criteria?
   - What players currently have no-trade clauses?
   - Let's look at the five top stars and what their bonus structures look like.

b) What criteria statements will you provide? What criteria will you not provide?
   Provide:
   - Let's look at Regina Miller's agreement: She gets a bonus for winning the championship, winning the MVP, and for games played.

   Don't provide:
   - None

4. Ready no-agreement alternatives

a) Will you disclose your BATNA? Yes, Kerry West has welcomed comparing Helen's other offers.

b) If you do disclose, how will you do it? Monique will share Helen's BATNA for comparison, not as a threat.

c) Will you ask about the other party's BATNA, and if so how? No, this doesn't seem helpful at this meeting. Monique may ask if negotiations get stalled.

QuickGuide for Step 2: Dig

Definition   The Dig step is where underlying interests are discovered.

Importance   This step gets parties to dig beneath their positions and to create value and expand the pie..

Preparation   Plan the questions you will ask regarding interests. Plan the statements regarding interests to be assertive and flexible.

Dialogue   Question: "Tell me more about your interests in quality."

                    Statement: "Here are my interests in the case. Most important to my client is that he is put into the same place he was before the incident happened."

Tips   Understand the other party's interests as thoroughly as possible. Share your interests as clearly as possible.

QuickGuide for Step 3: Develop

Definition   The Dig step is where options are brainstormed and narrowed through criteria and interests.

Importance   This step moves parties closer to agreement in a win-win fashion.

Preparation   Plan ways to get the other side to provide options. Prepare criteria statements and questions to narrow options.

Dialogue   Question: "Now that we've brainstormed ten different options, which two or three look promising enough to explore further?"

                    Statement: "Given the agreements the three neighboring communities have made, proposals two and six strike me as most in line with them."

Tips   Remember the shared, differing, and conflicting interests. Understand relevant criteria. Brainstorm options without commitment. Select options that may be agreeable to both parties.

YOUR NEGOTIATION WORKSHEET

Now return to your own negotiation. Write your answers to the Dig and Develop summary questions in the worksheet on the following pages.

Your Negotiation Worksheet

Dig and Develop Checklist

1. Discover interests

    a)   What questions will probe for the other party's interests?

    b)   What interests do you want to share? What interests do you *not* want to disclose?

2. Brainstorm options

    a)   What options might you try to draw out?

3. Narrow through criteria

a) What questions might you ask to find helpful criteria?

b) What criteria statements will you provide? What criteria will you not provide?

4. Ready no-agreement alternatives

a) Will you disclose your BATNA?

b) If you do disclose, how will you do it?

c) Will you ask about the other party's BATNA, and if so, how?

REVIEW (*SEE ANSWER KEY AT END OF CHAPTER*)

Check all that apply

1. The following are consequence questions:
   __ a) "What's the main problem you face in your business today?"
   __ b) "What's new in your department?"
   __ c) "Since you don't have a copy machine on-site, how do you get your copies made?"
   __ d) "Jacob, if your sister uses the computer for the next hour, what might you do instead?"

2. In dealing with a win-lose adversarial negotiator, consider the following approaches:
   __ a) Mirror difficult tactics.
   __ b) Blame the other person for his or her behavior.
   __ c) Continue to use a problem-solving approach.
   __ d) Understand the other person's behavior without excusing it.
   __ e) Help the other party understand your goals.

3. Ways to make it easier for the other party to share his or her BATNA in a constructive manner include:
   __ a) Articulate the goal of creating the best possible agreement.
   __ b) Acknowledge that not agreeing is a reality of negotiating.
   __ c) Threaten the other party with your BATNA.
   __ d) Tell the other party, "It's my way or the highway!"

True or False

__ 1. Be flexible with your interests and assertive with your options.
__ 2. Separating inventing options from deciding options can help generate creative solutions.

3. The BATNA tipping point is the point at which a party will not go to his or her BATNA.

   4. The Dig step is about narrowing and evaluating options.

   5. The Develop step is about brainstorming interests and no-agreement alternatives.

ANSWER KEY

Check all that apply

1. The following are consequence questions:
   a) No. "What's the main problem you face in your business today?" is a challenge question—a request to identify a problem. It does not ask for the impact of the challenge.
   b) No. "What's new in your department?" is a general question and does not get at the result of a challenge or a problem.
   c) Yes. "Since you don't have a copy machine on-site, how do you get your copies made?" asks for the aftermath or result of the challenge (of not having a copy machine).
   d) Yes. "Jacob, if your sister uses the computer for the next hour, what might you do instead?" gets at what will happen as a result of the challenge (of Jacob's sister using the computer).

2. In dealing with a win-lose adversarial negotiator, consider the following approaches:
   a) No. Mirroring difficult tactics often escalates the conflict. Differentiate this from being assertive or expressing concern about the impact of the behavior.
   b) No. Blaming the other person for his or her behavior can lead to a downward spiral similar to mirroring difficult tactics. Differentiate this from sharing concern about the impact of the other person's behavior.
   c) Yes. Continuing to use a problem-solving approach allows you not to be distracted from achieving substantive and relationship goals.

d) Yes. Understanding the other person's behavior without excusing it is like probing for underlying interests to create a better solution.

e) Yes. Helping the other party understand your goals helps him or her understand you, which may help the other party be more flexible and less positional or adversarial.

3. Ways to make it easier for the other party to share his or her BATNA in a constructive manner include:

a) Yes. Articulating the goal of creating the best possible agreement makes it clearer to the other party that sharing his or her BATNA may prompt new options that all parties might ultimately agree to.

b) Yes. Acknowledging that not agreeing is a reality of negotiating may help reduce the reluctance of the other party to share his BATNA for fear of upsetting you.

c) No. While threatening the other party with your BATNA may get the other party to share her BATNA, she is more likely to do so negatively.

d) No. This is the same as a threat. Telling the other party, "It's my way or the highway!" may get him to share his BATNA, but he is more likely to do so as he walks out the door.

True or False

1. To be true, this statement would read, "Be assertive with your interests and flexible with your options." Do not compromise on your primary interests. However, be open-minded about options that meet your interests.

2. Separating inventing from deciding options can help generate creative solutions because it helps parties brainstorm more freely.

3. False. At this point the party goes to his or her BATNA.

4. False. The Dig step is where you listen for and share interests.

5. False. The Develop step is for narrowing and evaluating options.

Step 4. Decide: Close the Negotiation

The 4D Decide Step *is about moving all parties toward yes or no in a wise and efficient manner without coercion. A yes means that parties will create as much value as possible. A no means that parties will go to their BATNA.*

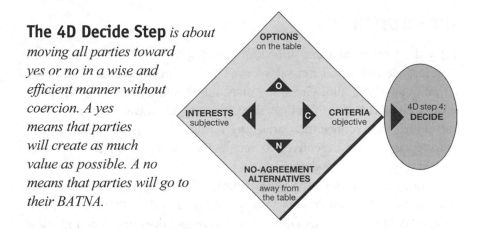

THE CHALLENGE

Lucy is a salesperson for Bauhouse Modern Furniture, which manufactures and sells high-end office and residential furniture. Richard is a buyer for DMC, the world's second-largest information technology company. DMC is looking to update the furniture in its offices around the world. Lucy and Richard have been negotiating over a three-month period and have worked through most of the issues. They craft a tentative agreement wherein DMC will purchase $4.2 million of furniture over the next five years at a heavily discounted rate.

Lucy expects that Bauhouse and DMC will sign the agreement at their next meeting. However, as they sit down together, Richard surprises

Lucy by saying, "Just one more thing before we wrap up: We need you to reduce the cost by 12 percent."

Lucy is shocked. "Richard," she says, "this is totally out of the blue! Why the sudden change?"

"Our third-quarter numbers went way below forecast," replies Richard. "And given the size of this deal, we thought you could do better."

"But I thought we had tentatively agreed to this contract," says Lucy.

"Yes, but it wasn't final. I talked to my boss, and she said we need something more to get the deal done. So what will it be? Do you want this deal or not?"

THE SOLUTION

Lucy does her homework prior to meeting with Richard. She discusses different scenarios with her sales VP, including one where DMC asks for an additional discount. Given the discounting applied thus far and their profitability analysis of this deal, they agree to walk away from it if necessary rather than reduce their price any further. They share their analysis with several other executives to secure their sign-off on this decision should it become necessary.

Lucy also reviews the other aspects of their agreement. Bauhouse will include DMC equipment in its advertising and marketing, and will switch its IT platform to DMC. The Bauhouse deal also has logistics/delivery cost savings for Richard's company. Teams from Bauhouse and DMC have worked long and hard to craft the best possible agreement.

"We want to reach an agreement with you," Lucy responds. "We would prefer to sign the papers today, but if there is a concern, then this may not be possible. Can you tell me whether your budget cuts are for this quarter, this year, or the entire five years of our proposed agreement?"

"We have a freeze for this quarter. Beyond that we don't know."

Taking her time, Lucy suggests, "One option, then, might be to change the up-front payment and delivery schedule to meet your immediate budget constraints. Depending on what happens, perhaps we can look at the remainder of the contract. If it's a total package issue, then one possible option might be to adjust the value of the contract relative to the reduction in cost."

Richard tries a different approach. "My CEO says we need this price cut to move forward. I don't think I can go back to him without some concession here," he says. "Maybe you need to talk to your VP or maybe even your CEO, given the size of this deal."

"We can get my VP on the line right now if you'd like," Lucy replies. "But our entire senior team has seen the analysis. We've worked hard to give you the best deal possible. If we need to look at the parameters again to see if we can create a better deal given the cost restrictions, I am certainly willing to put in the time and effort to do so. In the meantime, I put together this fact sheet on our tentative agreement. It outlines how you have a better discount rate than any other Bauhouse client, how we will use your products in our new ad campaign that begins next quarter, the logistics advantages to DMC, the IT platform sale for you, and so on. You are welcome to take a copy back to your CEO if it helps."

Richard leans back in his chair. "Okay, I will. Thank you. But Lucy, Just-Low Furniture is clearly cheaper than Bauhaus, and that's their primary advantage."

"Any cons going with J-Low?"

"They can't do the joint advertising."

"Do they use DMC for their IT platform?"

"They're considering it."

Lucy pauses. "Well, I would welcome talking further if that helps us move forward. But I'd like to be clear that these financials are the best we can do given our current agreement."

Overview: THE DECIDE STEP

Focusing on Decide

- Generates momentum
- Moves negotiation toward closure

Bottom Line

The Decide step moves parties toward yes in a wise and efficient manner and without coercion.

"I appreciate all the work and information that you passed along today," Richard says. "I'm going to have to check with my boss. I can't guarantee she will be convinced, but at least I can tell her we can begin an advertising campaign right away, and that I can say with certainty we have the best financials possible."

A week later, Lucy and Richard meet again, make a few adjustments to their agreement, and then sign it—the best possible agreement for both companies.

For many people, the Decide step is the most challenging part of a negotiation. Should I make an offer? Should I let the other side start? This question returns to the paradigm of positional bargaining. Yes, offers do have a psychological impact on the other party. They may anchor one party's thinking about what their counterpart is really willing to settle for. If you are unprepared, you are likely to react poorly to offers. Being strategic in the Decide step means using your knowledge to make wise decisions as you complete the negotiation.

It is important to be able to create momentum and move the other party and yourself toward closure. Making it easy for the other party to say yes rather than coercing him or her is key. This chapter is about how to move toward commitment wisely and efficiently.

I focus on three main tasks in the Decide step:

1. Aim for the Best Possible Agreement.
2. Make tentative agreements.
3. Take the next steps.

In each step, and just in case, be ready to go to your BATNA. As you conduct the negotiation and move to the Decide step, these strategies help move you toward final agreement.

THE AGREEMENT

Aim for the Best Possible Agreement

During the Decide step, continually target the Best Possible Agreement (BPA)—the ultimate win-win solution. You are squeezing the maximum value out of the negotiation, not concessions from the parties. Negotiators who put together strategic alliances between large companies use the BPA concept to measure how close they have come to achieving the ideal partnership. The closer the agreement is to the ideal, the more successful the alliance. If the agreement is only halfway to the target point, the partners are not in a win-win situation.

Leverage

Even in the most win-win negotiation, generally value has to be divided in negotiation. This is where leverage comes into play. Leverage is the power or ability to influence people and decisions. All the ICON concepts described serve as leverage. Traditionally in negotiation, we are more likely to consider forms that are viewed as more negative or unilateral in nature. So if one person is the boss and the other person is an employee, the boss's ability to fire the employee is a no-agreement alternative that is a form of leverage. An employee's leverage in a salary negotiation may be the fact that she has another job offer.

However, interests can serve as a positive form of leverage. If you are selling your house and want to get the maximum price, to sell quickly, and there is one Realtor who has sold more houses and at the highest average price in your neighborhood, the Realtor has a greater ability to meet your interests than other Realtors. If a pharmaceutical company can show unbiased studies that its drugs have a higher efficacy than those of its competitors, that gives the company leverage in negotiations. If a plaintiff is suing a defendant in a personal injury case and the 10 most similar cases resulted in a $2 million judgment on average, this criterion serves as leverage.

Pinpointing where you have leverage and where the other party has leverage in negotiations will reduce stress and pressure in negotiations. This will help you figure out ways to enhance your leverage and reduce the other side's strengths. Within a negotiation you can then also respond more effectively to your counterpart's moves that emphasize his power.

KNOW YOUR BOTTOM LINE

The Decide step of your negotiation may be less about achieving the best possible agreement and more about whether or not you should walk to your BATNA. Having a clear picture of your bottom line or minimum possible agreement will make you more decisive. Before you begin making decisions, knowing your bottom line will serve as a trigger point for whether the agreement at the table is sufficient. I have worked with organizations where identifying the Minimum Possible Agreement (MPA) was the key organizational competency to be enhanced. Sales professionals in the organization had no idea when an agreement was not good enough. Ultimately, this approach damaged their financial viability. By setting bottom lines for agreements, the sales professionals had clearer parameters, and profitability improved.

Make Tentative Agreements

It's important to make agreements on small and large issues as you go along—on specific issues like price, volume, delivery date, payment terms, and so on. It can be nearly impossible to come to agreement on all issues at once. The quandary is that it's often hard to make agreements on small issues when other issues loom large. To manage this challenge effectively, negotiators make tentative agreements contingent on the whole. This is a fancy way of saying that as you make agreements on any given issue, nothing is final until the parties see the entire agreement as a whole. The greater the number of issues involved, the more important this technique and your explicit use of it becomes (see the Cherry-Picking tactic in Chapter 9).

Because the negotiation landscape changes, you may occasionally find a need to reopen an issue that was previously decided. Circumstances may have changed, or new information may have come to light that makes your tentative agreement unfair or untenable. Exercise caution before reopening because doing so can increase distrust. Be as transparent as possible—explain your rationale and motives carefully. If the other party reopens, seek to understand her rationale and motives. Then share your needs. If there is a significant change, you might request that the whole agreement be looked at instead of just the issue being reopened (see the Another Bite of the Apple tactic in Chapter 9).

As you prepare for a negotiation meeting, jointly determine, if possible, what issues you may tentatively agree upon. If the parties have done their Dig and Develop work, possible tentative agreements should be clear. Tentative agreements can be reopened later in the negotiation because of what the agreement as a whole looks like. Ideally, since interests and criteria have been shared earlier in the negotiation, the other party understands why this is happening. Without explicitly using tentative agreements, reopening closed issues can be considered a "difficult tactic."

SHOULD YOU MAKE THE FIRST OFFER?

Being an effective negotiator means being a strong advocate as well. When it comes to cutting the pie, it is important to consider the offers and counteroffers. This is particularly true for negotiating issues with financial or other significant quantitative aspects. Assuming you have done your ICON work on the issue and have a good knowledge of the subject matter, then it makes good sense to make the first offer. When you want to shift expectations of the range of the agreement, being more aggressive in your offers may make sense.

Yes, you need to rely somewhat on offers to gauge what the possible agreement looks like, and yes, your offer may have a psychological impact on the other party's perception of what a possible agreement looks like (see the Smart Negotiator Tip on page 138). But the more you understand the ICON elements of any given issue and the better you have performed your Dig and Develop work, then the more you can reduce your reliance on offers as the measure of a possible agreement.

WHAT SHOULD YOUR FIRST OFFER BE?

The reality of negotiating is that the parties involved are advocates for their interests or the interests of their organization. It is important, therefore, to be assertive. Another reality is that every negotiation has give and take, so avoid haggling if you can: If you have agreed to a collaborative

---

Tactic Alert

The Flinch

No matter what offer you begin with, the other party reacts as if it is extreme. The goal of this tactic is for you to lower your aspirations and make larger concessions. If the other negotiator doesn't budge, learn more about her interests and criteria. You may also need to inform her of the criteria for your offer.

Tactic Alert

Take It or Leave It

In this tactic, one party demands that the other accept the offer on the table or end negotiations. This can be benign—an attempt to reveal their BATNA, or a reaction to something you said. It can also be an attempt to force you to capitulate. Explore your interests and options further; reaffirm the negotiation process. You might accept the offer with specific caveats or adjustments, or end negotiations and go to your own BATNA.

---

approach, then there's no need to start really high. Also, be wary of taking advantage of the other party in a negotiation. This isn't naive simpleton talk: Cheating others will usually come back to bite you, or worse, ruin you. Don't let yourself be cheated, either—know your interests. In any situation, the highest offer made in your negotiation should be the highest offer an outside party (after considering the relevant information) might judge as fair.

Imagine the Helen Hoops negotiation progressing. The team had concerns about Helen getting injured while riding her motorcycle. The parties discuss possible options and agree that Helen's agent, Monique, will craft a proposal that can be tentatively agreed upon. Monique's proposal is that Helen will not participate in motorcycle racing and will only ride recreationally if she wears full protective gear. With regard to Helen's leadership role with the team, different options are discussed—player-coach, captain, and spokesperson. Kerry, the team's general manager, takes the responsibility of offering a proposal to achieve a tentative agreement on this issue. In this way, each issue in turn can be discussed, tentatively agreed upon, and set aside.

WAYS TO GET TENTATIVE AGREEMENTS

Closing is a skill in many disciplines, and negotiation is no exception. The difference here, using the ICON negotiating model, is to use methods that focus on objectivity, choice, and fairness. A few methods that can lead to closure are described in the following list:

4D Key Point

Strive for a better deal for all parties as you get closer to final agreement.

- **Test the waters.** Think out loud (and frame it as such). Ask, "What if?" This is part brainstorming and part evaluation and is a way to reach closure. Primary interests often become clearer when you start test committing to options, and hidden interests sometimes become more obvious. "What if we use the folks in your organization to deal with that part of the project? It's where you have the most expertise. That way we can reduce the price to the range you're looking for."
- **Provide choices.** Giving people choices is a good idea, especially toward the end of a negotiation where it is easy to feel boxed in. Choices give freedom and power to the other party and help cement a sense of buy-in to the final agreement. "I could be happy with either option. Why don't you choose between these two packages?"
- **Use reciprocity.** See if the other party is willing to do the equivalent or reverse of what you are being asked to do. Let's say that Jacob runs a construction company, and he is building a house for

---

Tactic Alert

Absentee Decision Maker

When the wrong people are at the table, you can encounter the "my hands are tied" tactic. The people at the table may agree with you, but they say that other parties such as their boss or the board make the decisions. Find out as early as possible whether the person across the table from you has the authority your negotiation requires. You may need to be at the table with someone else, or you may need to design your negotiation to include input from other parties before a decision can be reached. Offer to help your counterpart persuade her internal decision makers.

Annie. Annie demands, "I want you to pay a penalty of $1,000 per day if you finish this project behind schedule!" Jacob responds, "I might be willing to accept that if I get a $1,000 per day bonus for finishing ahead of schedule."

- **Find a helper.** If the parties in a negotiation can't overcome their tendency to haggle or aren't making progress toward a decision, consider agreeing to a helper process that all parties in a negotiation perceive as fair—a mediator, arbitration, or a third-party expert opinion, for example. "We have been arguing about what to do with this chemical spill, and our agencies need to come to an agreement. We both respect Professor Lee at Purdue. What would you say to the idea of having him make this recommendation instead of each of us getting our own specialist?"
- **Split the difference.** Split the difference between reasonable criteria. This may seem concessional—like haggling—but there's a difference between splitting the difference between arbitrary numbers and splitting the difference between numbers and terms that parties see as reasonable. "Yes, I can understand the Forrester Group's analysis and how it determined the value. And I realize that you question the underlying assumptions of our independent researcher. Now that we both understand the pros and cons of each study, the fact of the matter is that the bottom-line difference is only 3 percent. That still translates into a fair amount of dollars, but I propose we split the difference, because we have spent resources examining and exploring and I think we both agree it's time to move forward."

Parties *will* get stuck when trying to make closure decisions—it's the nature of negotiation. Using these strategies can help; going back to interests can also be a good idea. Perhaps there's a major interest that hasn't been met yet. Perhaps a party hasn't been persuaded that the deal is fair and she or he needs to have a deeper discussion of criteria. Maybe a BATNA needs to be put on the table to reality-test whether an agreement can and should be made.

Certain negotiations may lend themselves to closure strategies that involve "cutting the pie." In *The Win-Win Solution*, authors Steven Brams

---

4D Key Point

When you get stuck, go back to underlying interests. Discipline, persistence, and patience will pay off.

---

and Alan Taylor present negotiation procedures to divide the value in ways that allow all parties to walk away satisfied—"divide and choose," "alternation," or "adjusted winner." In the divide-and-choose scenario, one party divides the pie, and the other party chooses which piece he or she would like. Under alternation, parties take turns choosing. With the adjusted winner format, each party is given a set number of points which he or she then allots to items on the negotiating table. Items are exchanged until each side possesses an equal number of points. Procedures like these can be useful in negotiations regarding a set of items to be divided between parties—in estate matters, for instance.

On the worksheet on the next page, practice closure strategies for your own negotiation. Pick one of the above strategies and then create sample dialogue to implement that strategy.

Take the Next Steps

At the end of a negotiation meeting there are a variety of small steps that can be completed to help make the next meeting more effective and move the parties toward closure. Identifying these steps, identifying deadlines, and designating responsibilities can all prevent pitfalls later on. These are steps that can be taken jointly or individually. Clarifying and committing to agenda items like timing and logistics, for example—the time and location of the next meeting—can create a placeholder for the negotiation that keeps momentum going. Agreeing on steps to communicate, inform, research, and consult—much of which is done away from the negotiating table—are also critical to many negotiations that require consensus-building. Parties might agree to prepare specific information for their next meeting, or look into a particular issue in more detail and report their findings for consideration prior to the next meeting.

Next steps are important even if you have achieved a final agreement and there will be no more negotiation meetings. They are crucial, after all, for ensuring and enhancing the proper follow-through on your agreement. An expert negotiator once told me, "The really important negotiation begins once you have the final agreement." The value of the agreement is not in the words, but in the actions that take place as a result of the agreement. The success of your agreement will still hinge on your ability to negotiate even after the "official" negotiation process is over.

4D Key Point

Remember to summarize your agreements.

Your Negotiation Worksheet

Closure Strategies

Closure Strategy _____

_____

_____

_____

_____

Sample Dialogue _____

_____

_____

_____

_____

_____

_____

Here are some possible next steps to move the Helen Hoops negotiation forward:

Next Steps

- Agreement to meet next Tuesday at owner's home in Lake Tahoe from 10 a.m. to 4 p.m.
- Kerry agrees to meet with owner before Tuesday meeting to discuss two specific issues.
- Monique agrees to bring her tax accountant to the meeting to focus on the best financial structure for an agreement.
- Kerry will bring attendance figures from last season to the meeting.
- Kerry's assistant will e-mail meeting notes to attendees.

BE READY TO GO TO YOUR BATNA

If and when you make the decision to go to your BATNA, do so in a way that reduces the negative impact. As discussed earlier, even raising your BATNA can be difficult. Convey your decision respectfully. A colleague of mine decided not to reach an agreement with a client. He was frustrated with how difficult a time he was having with the client's organization. He was both honest and sensitive in framing this to the client. "We have decided not to pursue a new contract with you," he said. "We will make sure that the transition is smooth, as you have been a valued client. The main reason is that we don't believe we can create the results we both want and need. We've discussed those challenges, and our belief is that our organization needs to take a new direction."

GETTING BOTH PARTIES ON THE SAME SIDE

The following advice is important for all steps of negotiation, and it is particularly critical throughout the Decide step. When parties are stressed and under pressure while making important decisions, the likelihood of contentious or adversarial behavior increases. Bill Ury, in *Getting Past No*, highlights the importance of building a "golden bridge" to the other party by respectfully acknowledging his comments and emotions even if you don't agree with his conclusions or solutions. The following are also steps that focus on getting both parties on the same side and moving the negotiation forward.

LOOK FOR VALUE IN THE OTHER PARTY'S OFFERS AND COMMENTS

Agree with the other party's points, if they are valid. Try to keep your dialogue "we" oriented rather than "us-them" so you don't create an oppositional conversation. For instance, suppose your counterpart offers the following: "I totally disagree with you. My team was totally disrespected. We contribute so much more to this project. Our folks put in more hours and weekends than anyone. That's why we need to renegotiate our share of the profits, which should go to 50 percent." How should you respond? There is anxiety and frustration in the other party's statement, so responding in-kind will only fan the flames. Saying, "That's a crock," for example, will only exacerbate the problem. So will saying something like, "My team has a lot more expertise and experience *and* it's providing the brainpower. Your team should get nowhere near 50 percent." A different response—one that might help build a bridge between negotiating parties—might be, "I agree. Your team *has* put in more hours and weekends. I would like to learn more about that issue, and really look at the numbers, rates, and other relevant factors for both teams."

ACKNOWLEDGE THEIR EMOTIONS

In one sense, a negotiation is people talking to each other trying to find creative solutions to issues. Sometimes these issues—as well as the people—are emotionally charged, yet we're often told (from our training and experience) that it's best to not show emotions in these settings. We aren't always accustomed, then, to dealing with strong emotions in a negotiation. While you don't need to become emotional in your negotiation or tolerate outbursts, simply showing awareness and recognition of emotions can improve the dynamic. It can show straightforwardness and remove an artificiality that can be characteristic of emotionally detached processes. Of course, don't psychoanalyze your counterparts and give them an explanation of why they might be upset—chances are you'll make things much worse! A better approach might be to say something like, "I could be entirely wrong here. Are you uncomfortable

People Skills
The Importance of Communication and Relationships

Negotiations are much easier when effective communication and an open relationship are present—issues can be discussed more openly and honestly. If these elements are missing, then having a straightforward conversation on interests, criteria, and options—not to mention on no-agreement alternatives—will be difficult. The following story shows how important communication and relationships are to bringing parties back to the table when negotiations have broken down and parties have walked to their BATNAs.

After F. W. de Klerk was elected president of South Africa in 1989, he took the incredible step of having the Government of South Africa finally recognize the African National Congress and release longtime political prisoner Nelson Mandela. The African National Congress and government of South Africa began talks to create a new constitution and government—no simple task given that South Africa's history included 50 years of racial apartheid. The bond forged between the two chief negotiators during these tumultuous and critical times reveals how important individual working relationships can be to a negotiation.

Cyril Ramaphosa was the chief negotiator for the ANC, and Roelf Meyer was the chief negotiator for the government of South Africa. They saw their jobs as opening the lines of communication without compromising on issues. Following the landmark agreement between the two groups, Ramaphosa and Meyer referred back to a fishing trip they had early on as a turning point in their relationship. A fishing hook had become stuck in Meyer's finger, which was bleeding profusely. Meyer trusted Ramaphosa to take the hook out. Meyer did recall being a little bit worried. "He had me take a drink of whiskey before he pulled it out. (Laugh) But he did it!"

In its own way, the fishing trip helped Ramaphosa and Meyer build rapport which would be called upon throughout the negotiations. The two of them had to deal with the fears and needs of all the people of South Africa. Many blacks abhorred the idea of working side by side with government officials, some of whom were the jailers

(*continued on next page*)

> *of dissidents like Mandela, while many in the white minority feared surrendering power to the black majority. The worst occurred when it came to light that some government officials from the white minority government had fueled the increasing black-on-black violence. Ramaphosa recalled, "There was a programmed agenda to destabilize the ANC." Negotiations stopped. Many on both sides thought that an agreement might not happen.*
>
> *Meyer, watching the national news on television, heard the broadcasters say that there was a "total breakdown of negotiation talks" and wondered what they would do next. Thirty minutes later, Meyer's phone rang. It was Ramaphosa. Meyer and Ramaphosa talked about what they would do to get things going in the right direction. The line of communication between the two of them became known as "The Channel" and continued to be the line of communication between ANC and the government when public channels were not working. The two sides eventually agreed to a historic new constitution and transition plan.*

Source: Roger Fisher. 1995 (video). *Five Skills for Getting a "Yes."* (Schaumburg, Ill.: Video Publishing House).

with something I said or did? Our joint goal is to work our problems out. I would hate to make things worse."

REFRAME NEGATIVITY IN A POSITIVE LIGHT

Negativity, criticism, and cynicism lead groups down the road to "us-them." Showing something in a positive light can change the dynamic of the negotiation. Imagine Nelson and Christina, co-owners of a bookstore, discussing what to do about an employee who handles their business affairs:

NELSON: We have to fire Jerry. He's just horrible at marketing. We should be doing much better.

CHRISTINA: Jerry's strength is clearly not marketing. I don't think he even enjoys it.

NELSON: We should hire someone else to do it.

CHRISTINA: That may make sense. But I believe Jerry does a great job of keeping the books, paying the bills, and managing all the money. Do you agree?

NELSON: Sure, but come on—he had specific goals for marketing, and he hasn't accomplished any of them.

CHRISTINA: You know, Jerry has mentioned on a couple occasions a desire to go part-time, so what if we peel off the marketing responsibilities and get a freelancer who specializes in that?

Christina reframes Nelson's negative comments in a constructive way. Doing so can turn around these types of situations and lead to good solutions instead of "us-them" reactions.

ASK FOR THE OTHER PERSON'S ADVICE

Why not ask your counterpart for advice on what you might do to move the negotiation forward? Asking for the other person's advice can be helpful on several levels. First, it creates an opportunity for agreement, if you heed the advice. Second, it shows respect for the person. Third, you are creating a coach/advocate role for your counterpart. Fourth, you get your counterpart to start to see things from your vantage point. Asking for advice sometimes leads people to stand in your shoes.

All of the above can be accomplished without conceding the substance of what you're negotiating. The main point to remember when you're trying to build bridges is to maintain a positive and constructive dynamic, particularly in the Decide step of a negotiation. At the same time, keep the substance and the relationship of your negotiation in balance. Working relationships often break down when parties attempt to reach closure—pressure and tension is often at its highest, even when both sides are well-intentioned. That's when it is critical to focus on the people side of the negotiation.

SMART NEGOTIATOR TIP

Drop and Counter Anchors

When making and receiving offers, keep in mind the effect of anchoring in order to be a better advocate. Exposure to even arbitrary or biased numbers changes a negotiator's assessment of what an agreement should be. Let's say that you walk into a jewelry store and ask to see something from the case. You glance at the price tag, and the seller immediately tells you that the price is actually half off what is marked. Without realizing it, you are likely already thinking how reasonably priced the jewelry is. When you get any offer, remember that this effect is happening to you whether you are conscious of anchoring or not.

Bazerman and Neale researched real estate listing offers as negotiation anchors. They varied the listing price but maintained the same information for all other data. Real estate agents then examined the actual houses and estimated appraised value, appropriate listing price, reasonable price, and lowest acceptable offer if they were the seller. The variation of the listing price had a huge impact on all four prices, specifically the higher the variation, the higher the estimate on all four prices. Interestingly, only 19 percent of the real estate agents indicated listing price as playing a big role in the assessment, and only 8 percent targeted listing price as one of the top three reasons for the estimated appraisal value.

As you are about to make an offer, recognize that you can shift the expectations of the other party. Be aware that when the other party makes an offer, the person may be attempting to shift your expectations as well. Even in collaborative negotiations, there is often value to be divided, and you are responsible for advocacy of your own interests.

SUMMARY AND DECIDE CHECKLIST

After you finish the Dig and Develop steps of your negotiation, use the following questions to help you plan your Decide step:

DECIDE: Create momentum and come to closure

1. **Aim for the Best Possible Agreement (BPA)**
   a) What is the Best Possible Agreement?
   b) What is your Minimum Possible Agreement?

2. **Make tentative agreements**
   a) What tentative agreements might you offer or accept in this meeting?

3. **Take the next steps**
   a) What are the next steps that will get you closer to an agreement on substance?

4. **Get both parties on the same side**
   a) What steps will you take to ensure that you and the other party are on the same side?

Review the example below from the Helen Hoops negotiation—the Decide Checklist for Helen's agent Monique.

Helen Hoops's Decide Checklist

1. Aim for the Best Possible Agreement (BPA)

   a) What is the Best Possible Agreement?
   - Multiple-year agreement at the same rate as the league's other top players, along with performance-based bonuses, no-trade clause, and a few perks
   b) What is your Minimum Possible Agreement?
   - One-year agreement at the same rate as the league's other top players, along with a no-trade clause

2. Make tentative agreements

   a) What tentative agreements might you offer or accept in this meeting?
   - Helen will not participate in motorcycle racing. She will wear full protective gear when she rides recreationally.
   - Captain of Golden Gaters

(continued on next page)

3. Take the next steps

a) What are the next steps that will get you closer to an agreement on substance?

- Agreement to meet next Tuesday at owner's home in Lake Tahoe from 10 a.m. to 4 p.m.
- Kerry agrees to meet with owner before Tuesday meeting to discuss two specific issues.
- Monique agrees to bring her tax accountant to the meeting to focus on the best financial structure for an agreement.
- Kerry will bring attendance figures from last season to the meeting.
- Kerry's assistant will e-mail meeting notes to attendees.

4. Get both parties on the same side

a) What steps will you take to ensure that you and the other party are on the same side?

- Helen will reiterate how she appreciates getting a better understanding of the team's perspective in this negotiation.

QuickGuide: The Decide Step

Definition	In the Decide step, we make agreements or walk to our BATNA.
Importance	Come to closure in this phase in a way that enhances the outcome and the relationship.
Preparation	Consider what offers you might make to achieve a tentative agreement contingent on the whole. Prepare possible next steps.
Dialogue	Question: "We've spent the last 30 minutes discussing the issue. Do you think we're ready to jointly create a proposal that we can both say yes to?"
	Statement: "I like the option you put forward for our final agreement. If we could address the interest I have in time urgency a little bit better, I'm ready to close on this issue."
Tips	Make it easy for the other party to say yes. Keep the conversation positive. Be up front about constraints.

YOUR NEGOTIATION WORKSHEET

For your own negotiation, answer the following questions to prepare for the closure phase of negotiation.

Your Negotiation Worksheet

Decide Checklist

1. Aim for the Best Possible Agreement (BPA)

a)   What is the Best Possible Agreement?

b)   What is your Minimum Possible Agreement?

2. Make tentative agreements

a)   What tentative agreements might you offer or accept in this meeting?

3. Take the next steps

a)   What are the next steps that will get you closer to an agreement on substance?

4. Get both parties on the same side

a)   What steps will you take to ensure that you and the other party are on the same side?

REVIEW *(SEE ANSWER KEY AT END OF CHAPTER)*

Check all that apply

1. Tentative agreements contingent on the whole are built directly from:
    __ a) Interests
    __ b) Criteria
    __ c) Options
    __ d) No-agreement alternatives
    __ e) None of the above

2. Using tentative agreements:
    __ a) Delays any decision making until the very end
    __ b) Protects you from negotiators who try to grab all they can in a negotiation
    __ c) Allows you to work with one issue at a time in a negotiation
    __ d) Makes every decision final
    __ e) Should be discussed in the Design step

3. The differences between tentative agreements and next steps include:
    __ a) Next steps are pieces of the contract or deal.
    __ b) Tentative agreements are agreements on things like when the next meeting will be, who will be consulted, and what research will be done before the next meeting.
    __ c) Tentative agreements concern all items that parties commit to doing as part of the final agreement.
    __ d) Next steps are often process-oriented—e.g., when and where parties will meet.

4. The next steps that can get you closer to the final yes in a cooperative manner include:
    __ a) Asking for the other party's advice
    __ b) Saying "take it or leave it"
    __ c) Acknowledging the other party's emotions

__ d) Reframing negativity in a positive light
   __ e) Looking for value in the other person's offers and comments

5. To close a negotiation cooperatively, you might:
   __ a) Split the difference
   __ b) Test the waters
   __ c) Make small concessions
   __ d) Unilaterally bring in another negotiator
   __ e) Provide choices

ANSWER KEY

Check all that apply

1. Tentative agreements contingent on the whole are built directly from:
   a) No. Tentative agreements do not need to be based on interests.
   b) No. Making tentative agreements does require narrowing and filtering through criteria.
   c) Yes. Tentative agreements are made on options or pieces of the proposal.
   d) No. You might compare a possible tentative agreement to your BATNA.
   e) No. Answer (*c*) applies.

2. Using tentative agreements:
   a) No. Agreements are made throughout. A final yes does come at the end. Tentative agreements, however, can be reopened.
   b) Yes. A main goal of using tentative agreements is to protect you from negotiators who try to grab all they can in a negotiation.
   c) Yes. A main benefit of using a tentative agreement approach is that it allows you to work with one issue at a time.

d) No. By definition, each decision is tentative. This does not mean issues can be easily reopened. Reopening should be done in light of the entire agreement.

e) Yes. Discussing this in the Design step allows parties to undertake a tentative agreement approach throughout Dig and Develop as well as the Decide steps.

3. The differences between tentative agreements and next steps include:
   a) No. Tentative agreements are pieces of the contract or deal.
   b) No. Next steps are these types of agreements.
   c) Yes. Tentative agreements concern items that are committed to within a final agreement.
   d) Yes. Next steps are process-oriented.

4. The next steps that can get you closer to the final yes in a cooperative manner include:
   a) Yes. Asking for the other party's advice helps reduce ego issues and helps create opportunity for agreement.
   b) No. Saying "Take it or leave it," usually seems adversarial.
   c) Yes. Acknowledging the other party's emotions may help improve the dynamic.
   d) Yes. Reframing negativity in a positive light is a great tool to keep moving toward agreement.
   e) Yes. Looking for value in the other person's offers and comments shows attention and respect that often builds relationship value.

5. To close a negotiation cooperatively, you might:
   a) Depends. Splitting the difference between arbitrary numbers is more like haggling. Splitting the difference between two objective benchmarks is more attuned to fairness.
   b) Yes. Testing the waters toward the end of a negotiation may help move you toward a final agreement.
   c) No. Making small concessions (and trying to extract larger ones) is more positional and arbitrary.

d) No. Unilaterally bringing in another negotiator will likely create suspicion and control. Discussing it beforehand and explaining the rationale would be a cooperative way of bringing in a new negotiator.

e) Yes. Providing choices is helpful in decision making. People don't like to feel forced to agree to a specific option.

PART THREE

BEFORE YOU GET TO THE TABLE

Part Three of this guide is the big finish—the extra heaping of whipped cream on the expanded pie. Here I offer a few vital, overarching thoughts on how you should prepare for and conduct any negotiation:

- Chapter 8: Strategize Fully
- Chapter 9: Deal with Difficult Tactics
- Chapter 10: Treat All Negotiations as Cross-Cultural
- Chapter 11: Act with a Clear Conscience

The theme for these chapters is to be prepared, flexible, and open-minded. A successful negotiation doesn't follow a recipe, but you should have the correct ingredients. Know what to expect, what needs to be done, and what you can and cannot do. With these final thoughts in mind, apply what you have learned in Parts One and Two of this guide to your next negotiation, and you can expand the substance and relationship value of any agreement.

8

Strategize Fully

To be successful at the negotiating table, effective negotiators consider the critical variants that influence negotiation outcomes. Understanding your style in negotiation will help you use your strengths and address your weaknesses. Considering the other's negotiation style will help you build rapport, frame issues, and move the negotiation toward an acceptable result. Identifying the type of negotiation you are entering will provide key information for you in choosing your style and approach. Choosing different modes of negotiation, for example, face-to-face, telephone, e-mail, and texting have advantages and disadvantages. You may benefit in certain negotiations by having an agent represent you. If you negotiate in teams, you will need to consider roles and expectations. Spending time imagining possible curve balls and worst-case scenarios will help keep you balanced in the face of any negotiation surprises.

UNDERSTAND AND DEVELOP YOUR STYLE

When you use the negotiation framework and the ideas presented here, adapting them to your own unique style as well as the people you are negotiating with is critical. Understanding and taking into account your degree of assertiveness and cooperativeness will help you plan and conduct your negotiations in a way that can leverage your own individual approach. Recognizing the other person's style will help you in framing what you do to be more persuasive, thus increasing your likelihood of success.

The style you use may change depending on the situation. The approach I use when I am bargaining with a potential buyer of two basketball game tickets is different from how I finalize child-care responsibilities with my wife. Some people may be more consistent across situations, while others may be competitive at work and more relationship-focused with family. Certainly your mood affects the style you show others. If you are happy, you might be more collaborative, whereas if you are anxious or fearful, you might be more zero-sum.

If we looked across your many interactions with others, you will likely find a vast array of approaches you have taken. As I introduce a framework for thinking about styles, it is important to remember not to pigeonhole yourself or others as showing only one style. In fact, improving as a negotiator may mean your working on a different style from the one you might otherwise take or eliciting a different style in your counterpart.

Most people have the capacity to be caring, adversarial, or withdrawn depending on a variety of circumstances. What may also be true is that you may default to one approach under pressure, which may be problematic and blocking you from getting better agreements.

Below are five approaches to negotiation, which are drawn from the work of Kenneth Thomas and Ralph Kilmann. As you read them, consider the following questions:

1. Which of these five approaches are you most likely to display in negotiation?
2. What are the pros and cons of each approach?
3. When are you likely to show each of these five approaches?
4. How would you deal with each of these approaches?

Approach 1: Competing

A person showing a competing tendency is focused on the substantive outcome of a negotiation more than the relationship. A competitor would assert his own interests and offer options that are more favorable to him. Other likely characteristics of this style include taking charge of a situation, a desire to win, enjoying partisanship, and a willingness to lead.

The advantages of a competing style are that individuals displaying this approach will likely be persistent in meeting their own goals and getting things done. The disadvantages of this style may be a higher likelihood of bruising relationships and a higher risk of deadlock in negotiations.

Approach 2: Accommodating

A person showing an accommodating tendency is focused on the relationship aspect of a negotiation more than the substantive outcome. An accommodator would empathize with her counterpart's interests and offer options that serve that person well. Other likely characteristics of this style include being supportive and helpful, wanting to be liked, a desire to preserve and foster good relationships, and receptiveness.

The advantages of the accommodating style are that individuals displaying this approach will likely build trust, create better relationships, and engender more positive feelings. The disadvantages of this style may be a higher likelihood of getting manipulated and taken, and making unjustified concessions.

Approach 3: Avoiding

A person showing an avoiding tendency is stepping back from the negotiation and is neither asserting nor cooperating. An avoider is not looking to resolve his own or the other's interests. Other likely characteristics of this style include patience, withdrawing from conflict, and reluctance to be too engaged or enthusiastic.

The advantages of the avoiding style are that individuals displaying this approach will likely avoid unnecessary conflict and take time to either emotionally cool off or think through the issues clearly. The disadvantages of this style may be a higher likelihood of issues not being addressed when they need to be and being perceived as aloof or arrogant.

Approach 4: Compromising

A person showing a compromising tendency is focused on the fairness of the resolution to both sides. A compromiser would stress criteria in negotiations and would not want to appear too self-interested. Other likely characteristics of this style include looking for expedient mutually acceptable solutions, pursuing efficiency, and wanting to appear reasonable.

An advantage of the compromising style is that individuals displaying this approach will likely resolve matters more quickly thus preventing needless time, energy, and emotion from being spent. The disadvantages of this style may be a lower likelihood of creativity and failure to deeply probe the issues.

Approach 5: Collaborating

A person showing a collaborating tendency is focused on creativity and problem solving. A collaborator would seek to generate new options that meet shared or dovetailed interests. Other likely characteristics of this style include probing for underlying concerns, a desire to enhance both the outcome and the relationship, and seeking mutually agreeable solutions.

The advantages of the collaborating style are that individuals displaying this approach will likely create mutually satisfying outcomes and relationships. They are more likely to create value and novel solutions. The disadvantages of this style may be a higher likelihood of increased time for negotiations and potentially annoying others and creating unnecessary issues.

Think through what happens when different styles mix with each other. For example, when a competing style meets an accommodating style, we might all anticipate the competitor taking advantage of the accommodator. This may in fact happen, but if someone feels she has been taken advantage of, she might also explode and respond in an adversarial, heated manner which might dramatically alter future negotiations and dynamics.

As you prepare for any negotiation, consider your own style and the natural strengths and weaknesses that flow from that. Consider different scenarios that may occur during the negotiation. What are difficult styles the other person might display? If you know the other person gets adversarial and competitive when he feels a lack of control, determine how to help that person maintain a sense of control. Recognize your own hot buttons and figure out ways to utilize style to your advantage rather than letting your emotions get the best of you.

While you are thinking about different people's styles, reflect on whether you want to change the dynamic by bringing a new party to the situation. Perhaps you just have not been able to build rapport with your counterpart. Consider bringing in a colleague who can utilize an accommodating style to build trust and a better relationship.

When you think about your own negotiation styles, ask yourself what style are you most likely to show under pressure. Also consider what style you want to work on enhancing.

IDENTIFY THE TYPE OF NEGOTIATION

How you make crucial strategic choices in a negotiation depends on the type of negotiation, specifically how much you value the substantive outcome and the relationship in any given situation. How I negotiate with my wife on dinner and a movie is different from how I negotiate with a client regarding the use of my company's intellectual property.

Richard Shell took the above thinking on negotiation style a step further. He categorized negotiations based on the perceived concern over the stakes and the perceived importance of the relationship between the parties (see Figure 8.1).

Every negotiation can be measured by the importance of the relationship and the substance. Knowing this will help you design your goals and approach in that specific situation.

Perceived Conflict over Stakes

		High	Low
Perceived Importance of Future Relationship between Parties	High	Balanced Concerns	Relationships
	Low	Transactions	Tacit Coordination

Figure 8.1 Situational Matrix
Source: Adapted from Shell: *Bargaining for Advantage.*

Tacit Cooperation

Tacit cooperation negotiations are those in which neither substance nor relationship matter greatly. An example of this is two strangers arriving at an entrance door of a building and figuring out who should go in first. Most people would be indifferent to whether they go first or second, and they do not have likely relationship interests either.

When faced with such a situation, avoiding or accommodating approaches make sense. One person either lets the other person go first or allows the other person the choice of going first or second. Certainly, people sometimes make the competitive choice and barge through first. That choice generally, though not always, will have few repercussions. Compromising and collaborating choices would be highly unusual, such as flipping a coin or engaging in a problem-solving discussion to figure out who should go first.

Transactions

Transactions are negotiations in which the substantive outcome is of high value and the perceived relationship value is low. The purchase of a car, office supplies, or a house would be situations in which you would prefer to get the best terms possible and in which typically you are less likely to have a long-term relationship. Such situations often involve negotiation between a seller and a buyer where price and other terms matter a great deal.

Be careful not to label a negotiation too quickly as a transaction. Even if it is a transaction, be careful to not choose a competitive approach as the only approach. A competitive approach would seem to be the natural response to such negotiations and that certainly makes sense. However, many negotiators too often fail to recognize the importance of rapport and trust-building in such situations. Sometimes, negotiators who choose a competitive approach are too rigid in doing so, and are overly aggressive. Credibility, likability, and honesty still play roles in transactional nego-tiations. I was at a house where the owner told me that he did not bid the highest price, but he and his wife wrote a letter to the owner stat-ing how much they loved the house, how they planned to raise their kids there, and how they would take good care of the residence. The seller, an older woman who had lived in the home for decades, had concerns before price that this couple hit upon and which distinguished them from other buyers.

Lawyers deal in transactional situations all the time, whether they are dealing with litigation or hammering out contract terms. An ability to be competitive, that is, assertive, and standing by your principles is critical, but much of what a lawyer does is compromise, not winning or losing all, but somewhere in between. Excellent lawyering also involves collaboration, the ability to problem solve. This approach ensures that whatever agreement is made is lived up to and meets the underlying interests of the parties. A colleague of mine was involved in a situation where a long-time loyal employee had suffered severe work-related injuries. When it came to dollars for settlement, the attorneys were very far apart. Only when the attorneys took a collaborative mindset did they come to agreement. The employee felt poorly treated once she reported her injuries to the company. Once the company's attorneys realized this, they offered the option of an apology from the company's CEO, which then moved the parties to a mutually satisfactory agreement.

Relationships

There are negotiations in which the parties perceive a high importance for the relationship and place a low value on the substantive stakes of the negotiation. For example, friendships and family are where such negotiations would occur.

An accommodating approach is important to take in such situations. Communicating clearly and building trust are skills practiced either too infrequently or too unskillfully. Within family and friend relationships, a number of barriers can prevent people from accommodating. Whether it is something psychological like ego or emotional like anger, challenges exist that stifle the desire to listen or please another person, even if there is little at stake. A husband and a wife argue about who is supposed to take the garbage out, but really the exchange is about something deeper within the relationship.

Just as for transactions, recognize that at times you may vary your response. Consider whether there are issues that matter. I remember a student who had a best friend who was constantly late. She was really bothered by her friend's tardiness, and it caused her both repressed anger and actual problems. However, she was not able to adopt any other approach but accommodating. She had to work on putting her own needs first which was very difficult for her in this relationship. She needed to do so to have a healthier long-term friendship.

Balanced Concerns

Balanced concerns are negotiations in which both relationship and substance matter. Classic examples involve coworkers, partnerships, and alliances. When an owner of a smaller business merges with an owner of a larger one, both obviously care greatly about the financial health for themselves individually and the new company as a whole. They also care about the working relationship they have, since they will be interacting together for years to come. These situations are arguably more challenging because of the tension between desiring a positive relationship and advocating for one's own needs.

Certainly, collaboration is a response that would make sense for such situations. Understanding the other side's interests, sharing your own, generating creative options, and sharing criteria that are persuasive all go to problem solving. Managing the communication and enhancing a positive sense of relationship go together with managing the substantive issues on the table.

YOUR NEGOTIATION WORKSHEET

Categories for the purpose of negotiation strategy are helpful to the extent that they sharpen your thinking and elicit effective actions that generate better results. Understanding the negotiation type will help you fashion your strategy. For your own negotiation, answer the following questions to prepare for different styles.

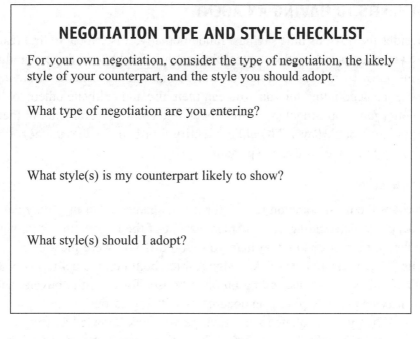

NEGOTIATION TYPE AND STYLE CHECKLIST

For your own negotiation, consider the type of negotiation, the likely style of your counterpart, and the style you should adopt.

What type of negotiation are you entering?

What style(s) is my counterpart likely to show?

What style(s) should I adopt?

WHAT TO DO WHEN THERE'S MORE THAN TWO

Most negotiations do not involve just the people at the table. You are often negotiating on behalf of someone else, or someone is negotiating for you. Lawyers, real estate and sports agents, investment bankers, accountants, and labor and management representatives are all examples of agents who are representing someone else in a negotiation. If you manage others, you likely face situations in which you will be managing and coaching your subordinates to negotiate on your or the organization's behalf.

Having someone else negotiate for you may be challenging if you are someone who is accustomed to getting things done on your own. The difference is that you must now enable others to be successful for the most part without your direct involvement in the negotiations. First, I identify benefits of having someone negotiate on your behalf. Second, I suggest things you can do to help the person negotiating for you.

BENEFITS TO HAVING AN AGENT

Besides the obvious time savings, fundamentally, it is critical to first realize you want people to do a better job than you would do in these negotiations. Only by acknowledging that can you realize the benefits of having someone negotiating for you. You can then hire and cultivate others to do a better job. Bob Mnookin, Scott Peppet, and Andrew Tulumello, in their negotiation book *Beyond Winning,* identify four benefits that the negotiator may have over you as the principal.

Knowledge

Perhaps the most common reason for using agents is that they may have a deeper understanding of a technical aspect of the negotiation (e.g., law, industry, market conditions) than you would if you were the sole negotiator. A real estate agent is knowledgeable about contractual terms with other real estate agents, setting up open houses for potential buyers, and identifying possible pitfalls in documents with the parties.

When you negotiate in areas where you lack knowledge, weigh for yourself the benefit of an agent's substantive issue expertise versus the cost. Consider the stakes and the time and effort for you to get up to speed and other ways of gaining the knowledge landscape necessary to succeed. Some people sell or buy their own houses by doing research and talking to agents and then doing it on their own.

Strategic Advantages

Let's say that you are in conflict with the other party. Having someone negotiate on your behalf may allow for a more collaborative result. On the other hand, having someone be more assertive in bargaining can help maintain your relationship. Agents are less likely to make concessions than principals. Be wary of how such strategy is implemented and perceived by the other party. It can backfire if not done well or seen well by the other party.

Many people find it hard to be objective when negotiating for themselves. They find themselves more stressed and therefore less effective. Such people can be too aggressive, too meek, or vulnerable to an emotional outburst. The classic example is hiring a divorce lawyer at a time when one is facing extreme changes in one's life accompanied by dramatic mood swings and external conflict. Agents can help depersonalize highly adversarial emotional negotiations.

At times, agents may be able to float ideas without commitment more easily than principals. If the principal suggests an idea just to explore it, the other side is more apt to glom onto it and less willing to let it go merely as a trial balloon. Another possible reason for an agent to suggest solutions is when an adversarial relationship exists between the principals. An agent can suggest an option without it being shot down immediately. This is called reactive devaluation and is covered in the box on page 112.

Resources

The negotiator may have access to resources and opportunities that would otherwise be unavailable. For example, the negotiator may have contact with a network of people that can provide information or introductions that you might not have. A sports agent will have relationships with general managers, sports marketing experts, other players, financial advisors, and others who can be extraordinarily helpful to a neophyte athlete.

Skills

Because of skills, background, or training, the person may be a better negotiator than you are. For example, you might have your HR person handle salary and benefits discussion, because she does it all the time and knows the ins and outs. Such a person knows what to avoid and what to pursue in a salary negotiation.

HOW YOU CAN HELP YOUR AGENT

The following are four things that I would suggest you do to help individuals who negotiate on your behalf.

Overcommunicate

A disadvantage of using an agent is the increased likelihood of miscommunication because of the additional layer within the negotiation dynamic. Spend lots of time listening. Especially if it is a new relationship, keeping each other in the loop is critical. Ask lots of questions. Use the opportunity to learn from your negotiators.

You and your negotiator will have different sets of "data." Exchanging information increases understanding and allows for mutual persuasion. Keep in mind that agents often fail because the principals are not sharing enough information or because they mischaracterize critical facts.

Manage the Process

Another disadvantage of using an agent is that the principal feels less in control of the process of the negotiation. Focusing on the results, looking at the pros and cons of different approaches, and not being stuck on one "right" way will allow your negotiators to increase confidence and comfort. Focus on how the negotiation might go, including how the negotiation would go ideally, and explore different possible scenarios and your responses to ensure that both agent and principal will feel ownership of the process.

Clarify Authority

Another possible disadvantage to using an agent is that agents may not do what you thought they would. Be clear on the parameters of decision making and authority. What is within the negotiator's authority to decide? What is not? Have this conversation before the person begins negotiating. This in and of itself is a negotiation. This is also called "negotiating inside out." The better your "internal" discussion, the better the outcome of the "external" negotiation will likely be. A bad result that often occurs is coming back to renegotiate because a person overstepped her boundaries.

AGENT-PRINCIPAL CHECKLIST

1. What are the advantages of having an agent?

2. What are the disadvantages of having an agent?

3. If you choose to use an agent, what will you do to ensure successful representation?

Align Interests

Be wary of agents who are too focused on their own interests. Because you and the individuals who negotiate on your behalf are different people with different positions, it is important to discuss what drives each of you. There are fundamental things like evaluations and salary structure that motivate agents. For example, a commission or bonus is a strong motivator for an agent. Things that motivate each of you include career, personal, and family goals. Being explicit with each other on your preferences and desires can help prevent distrust later.

TEAM NEGOTIATING

Instead of agents and principals, there are other times when there are multiple people on each of the sides. Team negotiating can be harder and more frustrating. Has a "teammate" ever said something that you thought totally inappropriate? Have you ever tripped over each other? Have your team negotiations ever seemed chaotic and disorganized? Have you ever felt uncomfortable saying certain things without your team's approval? What we don't tap into enough are the benefits of having a team when it comes to negotiation. The knowledge, the experience, the expertise, and the creativity can be fully released through focusing on a few key elements. I've worked with labor and management negotiation teams, teams from two organizations that were attempting a merger and account sales and purchasing teams. By focusing on these elements, they were more able to navigate through difficult negotiation terrain.

Prepare

There is no substitute for preparation. Certainly everyone's busy. And the more people involved, the more difficult it is to find time to prepare. Yet the more critical the negotiation is, the more important it is to spend quality time getting ready. Unfortunately, teams that spend time in preparation often do not use their time wisely. Like actors or athletes, once they've done their preparation, they're ready for anything. The same is true for negotiators. Here's what you should do in preparation.

Set Team Goals and Work Backwards

What is the team trying to accomplish? Visualize the negotiation coming to end and that all parties are satisfied. What are the outcomes and the results? From the goals, you can then work backwards to what needs to be done to be ready.

What are the tangible or deliverables? For example, you may be trying to get a contract or a list of action steps. This will also help the team realize what else is needed.

What information or expertise is needed to help you get to the goals? Maybe you need certain statistics or financial or legal expertise in the room.

What is the decision-making process? This is important both within your team and between the teams. How will your team make decisions? It may be by consensus or by the team leader. The important thing is working this out beforehand.

How will you handle intrateam conflict? The better your team negotiates "internally," the better your team will conduct its "external" negotiation. I've seen successful teams have internal agreements on how they will handle disagreements. They agreed to check in at the end of each meeting or even in some cases take a break so that the teams could caucus.

What are the roles that each team member will play? This is absolutely key, especially for teams that are newly formed. Having "purposive" roles provides each person with something specific to do. More preparation and work can thus be shared. Some possible roles include who takes the lead on specific issues, a note-taker, a facilitator, and an observer. A word on observers; if you have a large number of people on the team, it could be very helpful to have a person really focused on listening and paying attention to the ebb and flow of negotiation. The person can then really zoom in on getting insight that might help the negotiation. The most famous negotiation team roles are certainly "good cop" and "bad cop" which are discussed in the sidebar "Rethinking Good Cop/Bad Cop." But try to think beyond famous roles to what different roles can do for you.

Role-Play

In the *Star Trek* television series, the "holo-deck" allowed the crew to simulate situations they were about to enter. The best preparation for a

(continues on page 164)

Rethinking Good Cop/Bad Cop

Maybe the oldest team negotiation trick in the book is good cop/bad cop. If nowhere else, we see it play out in movies and on television where during an interrogation of the alleged suspect, one officer berates the person, throws a chair, and has to be restrained by (stereotypically) his partner. The "bad" cop then leaves the interrogation room. The "good" cop then gives the suspect a cup of water and says, "I don't know if I can hold off my partner for much longer, so you better tell us what you know."

Does this tactic work? Sometimes, sure. Can it backfire? Absolutely. If the other team suspects this trick, trust will disappear faster than a magician's rabbit. Let's try to understand why this tactic might work, how to defuse this tactic if your team faces it, and what roles your team might utilize instead.

First of all, good cop/bad cop is easy to do. One person solely pushes the other side to the limit without ever having to worry about giving in. The other person just has to be polite and accommodating without having to think about being aggressive. When it works, it allows the team to get what they want while maintaining a positive relationship (at least with the good cop).

If your team faces this, you have a number of options at your disposal. Just being aware that the other team might use this tactic should defuse any of its effectiveness. Also, the team can just "name" it to the other team. I have seen teams just point out in a joking fashion the dynamic and it changed how the other team approached the negotiation. Another way is to deal forthrightly with the "bad" cop. Letting the other team know that the threat would not work, that is, that they were more than willing to walk away from the table and that there were other means of getting their needs met, often reduced the effectiveness of such tactic. Regardless, the team should discuss and determine their strategy as much as possible.

In terms of creating roles on your own team, what we can learn from good cop/bad cop is that it is important to be both assertive and empathetic in negotiations. But roles do not have to be caricatures, and nobody needs to be locked in to play one type or another. Have the team explicitly discuss how they will create a positive relationship and how they will actually get there combined with understanding the critical interests in the substantive issues. Designating people to take the lead on substantive issues and being assertive on key issues can be useful without precluding others from doing so as well. Also having people on the team with good people skills is important without precluding the idea that everyone can be focused on building a positive relationship. Creating a collaborative rather than a coercive dynamic calls for people to be three-dimensional rather than cardboard figures.

TEAM PREPARATION CHECKLIST

1. *What is the team trying to accomplish?* The absolute first priority is to set team goals and work backwards. Visualize the negotiation coming to an end and that all parties are satisfied. Perhaps the overall purpose includes a win-win deal and a better working partnership. You can then conceptualize what is entailed for you to be successful.

2. *What are the deliverables?* Given the team's overarching goals, figure out the tangibles or concrete things that will be accomplished during the negotiations. For example, you may be trying to get a contract or a list of agreed-upon action steps.

3. *What information or expertise is needed to help you reach these goals?* Given the above, you may need to have certain financial, legal, or other expertise available (or in the room).

4. *How will your team make decisions?* Be clear up front on how decisions will be reached, whether one person will have sole decision-making ability or whether the team operates by consensus or something in between.

---

difficult situation is to practice it, and as closely as possible, approximate the actual environment. Lawyers who prepare to argue their case actually practice and have others play the role of judge, jury, and opposing counsel. In my consulting work with negotiation teams, I will have the team role-play possible scenarios. The goal is not to create a script, but to create a comfort level with what might actually happen.

FIGURE OUT HOW TO COMMUNICATE

An important choice to make is what mode of communication you will use to negotiate. Too often, people choose based less on what will bring about the best outcome; they prefer the path of least resistance. If the person is a conflict avoider, that person may likely choose e-mail or calling at an hour when he is reasonably sure the other person will not be available. An accommodator might prefer a face-to-face meeting to work on building the relationship.

Certainly prioritization and efficiency matter as well. If the negotiation result is not important, then it makes little sense to drive 50 miles to meet face-to-face at a restaurant. If you have an excellent relationship with the other negotiator, you can possibly raise a sensitive topic in a phone conversation.

Face-to-Face

The advantages of face-to-face communication are numerous. If you are dealing with complex substantive and emotional issues, then face-to-face is often the best call for managing the subtleties, intricacies, and challenges involved. If rapport and trust are important, then having the availability of body language and facial expression is critical. From a persuasion perspective, you have more impact in influencing the dynamic between the parties. If you want to create a comfortable and quiet environment, by meeting in person you can exert much more influence. In any other medium, the other party chooses the place he or she occupies.

The disadvantages are that meeting face-to-face may set fire to a flammable situation; that is to say, a face-to-face meeting can escalate preexisting conflict. People's hot buttons may get pushed more, and some people are more stressed if they are meeting face-to-face. Some may be at more risk to concede in the face of intimidation or guilt-inducing tactics. Many people find it easier to end a phone call or text conversation than when they are in each other's physical presence. Other negotiation media provide more time to reflect before responding.

Phone

A phone call allows for all the wonderful qualities of the voice to come into play. Volume, tone, and pace all matter. Certainly for simpler or reduced scope negotiations, this is a great approach. Generally speaking, a phone call is much easier to schedule and make happen than face-to-face meetings are. It therefore has advantages for negotiations that are time sensitive, where meeting is not practical, or where the issues to be discussed are relatively minor. For psychological and pragmatic reasons, phone negotiations are easier to end. For people who are more accommodating, it may be easier to maintain one's strategy rather than conceding. Because there is less stimuli, it may be easier for some to focus on the specific issues to be discussed rather than be distracted.

A discussion of disadvantages of phone negotiations begins with the lack of control over the other person's environment and the risk of a bad connection, especially when cell phones are used. The other person may be multitasking, thus creating a greater risk of miscommunication. Interestingly, people who are milder interpersonally may be more likely to show anger on a more removed mode like phone than in a face-to-face situation. To deal with the disadvantages, you can certainly manage your own environment well by choosing a quiet private place and where your line will be clear. You can do more to influence the other person's environment by finding a time when the other person will be in an environment conducive to having a phone conversation. Certainly call for a break if you sense the onset of challenging emotions and check whether all the parties are adequately prepared and monitor whether delaying the negotiation will yield better results.

E-mail

One of the biggest benefits of e-mail is its asynchronous nature. You have time to think about your response. You can prepare, research, and get coaching between responses. It can be useful for both highly complex negotiations as well as transactional and simple negotiations. For low-importance negotiations, this is a quick way of handling such matters. If you have an excellent relationship with the other party, e-mail is an efficient way to deal with small or reduced-scope matters. For transactional negotiations, it allows for easier advocacy, especially if you have an excellent walkaway.

One disadvantage is that e-mail is less useful for negotiations with a high degree of emotion or conflict involved, even less so than using the phone. Unfortunately, another big downside of e-mail is that an individual in the privacy of her bedroom or cubicle knocks out an e-mail in a moment of passion and hits send before taking a moment to cool off and reflect in a detached way. The person might never have made those comments face-to-face, but in the anonymity of solitude, easily does so.

Certainly common sense dictates reviewing your e-mail before sending it. Saving a draft and stepping away from the e-mail can give you necessary distance to focus on how the other person will receive it. Edit it by focusing on the impact it will have on the recipient rather than your intent when you wrote it. For important negotiation e-mails, have another person read it prior to sending.

Texting

Texting or instant messaging can certainly be helpful for urgent time-sensitive matters. Given the preference for some who use texting, it can be helpful in building rapport and connection. However, at this point I would be very cautious in using it for negotiation. By nature, people are often distracted and multitasking when they are texting. Messages tend to be ultrabrief in length and curt in tone. For these reasons, texting magnifies the disadvantages of e-mail for negotiation while not necessarily leveraging e-mail's advantages. When you are texting from a smartphone rather than a computer, you may be less likely to take the time to reflect and research before responding as you might in e-mails.

While you may want to text because of your or the other party's preference for its usage, be judicious in what issues you raise and discuss in text. Topics that are subject to multiple interpretations are not useful for this medium. Like e-mail, text communication is not ideal for dealing with challenging emotions. Stick to simple and discrete statements and questions, and reserve complex issues for a different medium.

Videoconferencing

High-end videoconferencing technology offers many of the advantages of face-to-face negotiation. The ability to deal with complex issues and emotions, the opportunity to provide and read nonverbal cues, and the chance to build relationships exist in this approach. Now people who are thousands of miles apart who could not practically do face-to-face negotiations can reap advantages that were previously unimaginable. Even for those who travel long distances, not having to do so can reduce the wear and tear on their bodies and possibly allow the parties to be less stressed in negotiations.

Other possible advantages for negotiators of videoconferencing over face-to-face are that they may be more comfortable in their own environment and can scan their notes more without feeling self-conscious about it. Negotiators who have trouble holding firm in face-to-face negotiation may find it easier to do so via videoconferencing. However, consider that live theater provides a different experience from even the highest definition cinema experience. In the same way, two people sitting next to each other have greater superiority than even the latest high-tech equipment. Recent neuroscience research also indicates certain physiological responses related to collaboration that exist only when people are in each other's physical presence.

The best technology is still expensive and may not be accessible. Some of the technology still suffers from connection speech and audiovisual quality issues. When using personal computers and Webcams, it is important to create the best possible picture and sound and prepare assiduously beforehand. For example, the computer screen and the Webcam need to be positioned so that you make eye contact by looking directly into the camera. Otherwise, the person does not see your face, and this can be alienating. Good lighting is critical as well. These points sound minor, but they actually make a huge difference in the feeling of connection. I would argue against using videoconferencing for high-stakes negotiations if the parties are not accustomed to its usage or if the audiovisual quality suffers or may fail.

Dealing with Difficult Tactics

Inevitably, you will run into behavior that pushes your buttons. Conflict will occur in almost any negotiation. Too often, though, individuals feel forced into a corner when this happens, which reduces their ability to respond thoughtfully and effectively. In reality, you have a lot of choices; the challenge is being able to see conflict as a chance to make things better, to create value, and to solve a problem.

STRATEGIES FOR DEALING WITH DIFFICULT TACTICS

This chapter offers strategies to deal with difficult tactics in a way that takes into account your reaction, and your goals. Think of it as a mindset you can use to minimize difficult tactics. The goal is to help you stand up for yourself, get the results you want, and decrease negative conflict.

Step 1: Increase Your Personal Awareness

Pay attention to your thoughts and feelings. Figure out what's bothering you. Is there an ego issue? Do you feel disrespected? Difficult tactics are much easier to handle if you are aware of what pushes your buttons and your reaction to this stimulus. Negotiations can be stressful, and when you're paying attention to the issues and concerns of other parties but not to yourself, you can get increasingly frustrated. You may not realize it until much later. Knowing yourself will allow you to make the right choices and help all the parties reach a strong agreement.

Step 2: Keep Your Eyes on the Prize

It's easy to lose sight of your goals when you get frustrated. That's when it's most important to remember your goals and your common ground—your shared interests. Does this mean you should ignore your feelings? No. Because you are aware of them, you can choose a strategy to manage them as you stay focused on your goal.

Step 3: See Yourself as Difficult

Remember the times when you have been difficult or irrational? In those situations, what did people say or do that helped you? Keep that empathetic mindset, and then try to understand the motivation or rationale for the other person's behavior. Somehow, the person across the table from you—no matter how irrational you think he is—feels that his actions and words are justified. What worked for you when you were being difficult may not work with this person, but finding a path out of contention requires understanding and empathy. This is harder to find when emotions are running high, so you will help lead the way by remaining calm.

CHOICES FOR DEALING WITH DIFFICULT TACTICS

Once you have made it through the three initial steps, you can evaluate your choices for dealing with difficult tactics.

Discuss It

There is power in "naming" a difficult tactic to the other person that can often stop the behavior. Share what's happening. Focus on the impact of the behavior. Rather than impugning the other party's intent, ask her to share why she did what she did. Ask if there's a problem that led her to act this way, or make a suggestion of how to proceed differently.

It's easy to start blaming the other side by saying things like, "You're causing this negotiation to fail!" However, this can lead to a downward spiral of accusations. A more positive approach is something like, "I'm starting to get frustrated on this issue. I've put several ideas on the table, but you've only expressed to me what's wrong with them. I'd like to understand what characteristics you think a good option should have.

Maybe we could put together a list of different options without evaluating them yet. Then we could go through them, focus on the merits of each one, and maybe find a great option from there. What do you think?"

Ignore It

Ignoring the tactic may be useful as well. Pretend it never happened, and stay positive. If it comes up again, use a different strategy. This can be disarming, if it is done well. You're saying, "What you are doing has no effect." Remember that you only control your own actions and no one else's. If the tactic continues to come up or if it bothers you, then discussing it may be the right call. It's easier to use this strategy if you have a powerful BATNA, since at some point, if the behavior persists, you can walk away from the table.

Deal with the Issue Later

In an ideal world, difficult tactics would always be discussed on the spot. However, negotiation rarely takes place in the ideal world. Sometimes you're caught off guard. Reflecting before speaking out about a difficult issue can be useful. Maybe you want to run your response by someone first. You can then test the accuracy of your perceptions and the impact of your response. Once you have had a chance to reflect, you can raise the issue in the same meeting or during the next meeting. Raising a difficult issue later may be easier when parties are refreshed and emotions are not running as high.

Leave

Staying in a bad situation isn't good for anyone. Exit the situation, if it makes sense. If it's for the short term, then leaving may give all the parties time to cool off and reflect. Go to lunch. Request to adjourn for the day. Often, taking the time to sleep on it and develop a different perspective is crucial to problem solving in a negotiation. If you're going to leave the negotiation for good, then make sure you've looked hard at your no-agreement alternatives and have a good BATNA. In either case, you may be best served by clearly explaining your intent—walking away doesn't have to mean burning your bridges.

Play the Game

On the other hand, there are instances—particularly in low-value negotia-tions—where it may be more efficient to simply "play the game" to get the desired outcome—to simply haggle if that's a choice or walk away. This scenario is described later in this chapter under the Old Dog tactic.

Use Appropriate Humor

Humor can make it easier for individuals to let their guard down—it can be very humanizing. Therefore, if the personalities and the situation are appropriate, humor can be a great tool for changing the dynamic of a nego-tiation. It can put parties at ease, cushion a hard message, and turn around a bad situation. Making light of a tactic can also help the other party see your interaction as being between individuals instead of negotiators, and it can get people to stop using manipulative tactics that arise from roles or stress. For instance, a colleague saw a good cop/bad cop routine start to emerge in a critical negotiation. "I feel like we're in a scene from a police drama," he said, "where one of you is being tough, and the other one is trying to be reasonable. I feel like I should say 'I admit it! I admit it! I broke into that bank!'" The colleague said that his negotiation counter-parts got a good laugh and they actually proceeded differently—and more constructively—from that point forward.

ENCYCLOPEDIA OF TACTICS

The Tactic Alert boxes throughout Part Two of this guide contain a few of the more popular negotiation tactics I've encountered in my work over the years. These are repeated on the following pages for your convenience, along with other tactics I've witnessed. The bullet points under each tactic are possible responses for dealing with it effectively.

Tactic Alerts

You will note that the responses I suggest are mostly ICON- and 4D-oriented. Depending on the specific circumstances you encounter, you may also want to incorporate some of the response strategies mentioned above, such as ignoring the tactic or dealing with it later.

The Haggle

Haggling happens when one party opens a negotiation by making an extreme or unreasonable offer and concedes sparingly while trying to obtain a more generous concession from you. Other tactics are sometimes used in combination with this one, such as "take it or leave it."

Effective responses to this tactic include:

- Deal with the haggle by jointly discussing how to approach the negotiation (a preventive measure).
- Ask for interests early and often, and remember to share yours.
- Brainstorm options before evaluating them.
- Prepare your BATNA.

Another Bite of the Apple

This tactic occurs when you are negotiating issue by issue and the other negotiator reopens discussions on a "closed" issue. There are legitimate reasons for reopening issues, but sometimes this action is a difficult tactic.

Effective responses to this tactic include:

- Use the tentative agreement approach and jointly decide ahead of time that if someone wants to reopen an issue, he or she will need to make a persuasive argument for doing so.
- Spend time understanding why the issue is being reopened.
- Understand the other party's interests.
- Share your interests, as well as your constraints.
- Agree that if changed circumstances are the cause of reopening, verification will be required as needed.

Cherry-Picking

This tactic occurs when you are negotiating issue by issue and the other negotiator tries to maximize his or her "take" on each issue without regard to the whole agreement.

Effective responses to this tactic include:

- Be clear during the Design step that you are making tentative agreements contingent on the whole to help prevent cherry-picking.
- Point out this behavior if you see it emerge, so you can keep the negotiation on track.
- Explain the links you see between key issues, and discuss these in relation to interests and criteria.
- Evaluate the agreement as a whole during your negotiation.

Chicken Little

We see it in the news every day: Party X says the sky is falling, and Party Y says it's fine. Both sides amass an impressive array of "facts," yet neither is listening. Debate rather than true dialogue is taking place. How can the wheat be separated from the chaff? Not easily, and sometimes not at all if facts are bent with the intent of supporting interests. Just as you can be positional with options, you can be positional with criteria.

Effective responses to this tactic include:

- Seek to understand criteria without necessarily agreeing.
- Return to interests to probe more deeply.

Hoarding

Hoarding happens when a negotiator latches onto any idea you put out there. This dynamic makes it difficult for you to discuss a range of ideas and proposals.

Effective responses to this tactic include:

- Before you negotiate, agree that the two of you are brainstorming—that you are inventing options at this stage, not deciding.
- If the other party starts to latch onto ideas, remind him or her that you are not offering these ideas for commitment.

The Flinch

No matter what offer you begin with, the other party reacts as if it is extreme. The goal of this tactic is for you to lower your aspirations and make larger concessions.

Effective responses to this tactic include:

- If the other negotiator doesn't budge, learn more about her interests and criteria.
- You may also need to inform her of the criteria for your offer.

Take It or Leave It

In this tactic, one party demands that the other accept the offer on the table or end negotiations. This can be benign—an attempt to reveal their BATNA, or a reaction to something you said. It can also be an attempt to force you to capitulate.

Effective responses to this tactic include:

- Explore your interests and options further; reaffirm the negotiation process.
- You might accept the offer with specific caveats or adjustments.
- You might end negotiations and go to your own BATNA.

Absentee Decision Maker

When the wrong people are at the table, you can encounter this "my hands are tied" tactic. The people at the table may agree with you, but they say that other parties such as their boss or the board make the decisions.

Effective responses to this tactic include:

- Find out as early as possible whether the person across the table from you has the authority your negotiation requires.
- You may need to be at the table with someone else, or you may need to design your negotiation to include input from other parties before a decision can be reached.
- Offer to help your counterpart persuade her internal decision makers.

The Old Dog

This is an inflexible negotiator who won't change—who won't learn new tricks. Often this person's only approach to negotiation is concessional.

Effective responses to this tactic include:

- Try to figure this out beforehand so you can decide how to negotiate.
- You can choose to not play the game. Don't commit if the offer on the table doesn't meet your interests. Strengthen your BATNA and be willing to walk to it.
- Play the haggling game—know your goals and your limits so the old dog can't take advantage of you.
- With the old dog, build wiggle room into your limits so that this negotiator can feel like he's "won."

Start from Scratch

You negotiate for months and agree in principle, but at some point the other negotiator wants to start all over again and take advantage of what has been learned and given up by you.

Effective responses to this tactic include:

- Understand your BATNA and improve it, if possible.
- If your BATNA is strong, reveal it.
- Align your internal team to support you.
- Change the player on the other side, or bring in additional parties.
- Keep price tied to value to avoid making costly concessions.
- Avoid concessions that are not reciprocated.
- Avoid making price the final item to be negotiated.
- Focus on the long-term advantages of the deal.

Just One More Thing

In what you believe is the final agreement meeting, your counterpart demands a large concession before signing (usually a monetary issue). This tactic is used to catch you off guard and take advantage of the fact that you expect and want to come to closure.

Effective responses to this tactic include:

- Ask questions to understand your counterpart's interests.
- Help her understand the cost of walking to her BATNA (loss of time and relationship) and reveal yours (if strong).
- Align your own team in order to assess support for the deal as negotiated.

Fait Accompli

This tactic occurs when the negotiator tells you that the decision has already been made on his side. He does this to get the agreement on his terms.

Effective responses to this tactic include:

- Design the negotiation process to build in communication and consultation before decision making (a preventive action).
- Dig for any interests that are met by this tactic, especially the client's internal interests.
- Assert that the matter under consideration is for joint decision making rather than unilateral moves.
- Strengthen and walk to your BATNA.

Insufficient RAM

You and your counterpart reach an agreement, but you both remember it differently because neither of you wrote it down. You suspect deception, but it may be a simple case of miscommunication.

Effective responses to this tactic include:

- Write down agreements in a public fashion—flip charts, papers, and so on.
- Send follow-up memos after meetings (a preventive action), and invite input for clarification.

- Ask for the other person's recollection, and share yours.
- If the problem persists, identify it to the other party as a tactic you perceive.

Auction Fever

Manipulative negotiators often try to get you increasingly committed to a plan of action while carefully limiting their own commitment. They make you feel trapped and thus get you to negotiate against yourself. This tactic contains parallels to the frenzied bidding at an auction: Bids go up, but intrinsic value does not change.

Effective responses to this tactic include:

- Name the game early.
- Know your limits.
- Research BATNAs with precision.
- Understand the interests and criteria of the other side.
- Don't make decisions based on sunk costs, but on future gains or losses.
- Develop problem-solving options, and defer any commitment until you have agreement on the whole.
- Decide on an issue-by-issue basis whether or not an agreed-upon option is acceptable. Don't proceed unless it is.

Do Me a Favor

Negotiators often make concessions to each other as they negotiate and implement a deal—consider these favors. Often parties place different values on these favors, assuming that trust exists and that their valuation is fair. When it comes time to cash in a favor you did for the other party, she discounts its value or acts as if you never did it. Your prior concession becomes worthless.

Effective responses to this tactic include:

- Avoid the unilateral concession style of negotiating (a preventive measure).

- Ask how the other side measures or values a favor you are making that benefits it.
- Keep a jointly written record of favors and the agreed value of each favor.
- Apply the test of reciprocity—exchange the favor for something of equal value.
- Turn a favor down, explain why, and offer a different option.
- Remind the other side that, "Nothing is agreed until everything is agreed" (mention tentative agreements contingent on the whole).

Good Cop/Bad Cop

This tactic is one of the classics. The person you are negotiating with develops a warm relationship with you, but he requires input from a hard-nosed partner who uses (or is said to be using—sometimes you never meet this person) coercive pressure. The buddy's role is to persuade and influence you to just go along with his slightly hard-line but allegedly fair partner.

Effective responses to this tactic include:

- Identify this tactic when it occurs.
- Bring additional members to your team to even the personnel ledger.
- Stay focused on ICON and resist coercive pressure.
- Separate the substance from the relationship—deal with each on its own merits.

As you can see, you can handle all these tactics strategically. Often the groundwork you lay in your preparation can head off the tactic before it begins.

Treat All Negotiations as Cross-Cultural

Throughout this guide I have touched on the importance of people skills and relationship-building. This is critical in negotiation because each of us is different. Each of us has a unique background and different experiences that play out when we negotiate. These differences include (but certainly aren't limited to) where we grew up, where we work, our school history, and the people in our lives. Even in the same family, a mother's experience and her daughter's may be quite different and so they may be negotiating across a cultural gap.

When negotiations break down—regardless of how different the parties are—the cause is often not these differences themselves, but the misunderstanding and miscommunication that comes from not being able to see the world through the other party's eyes. Why not bring the positive, open-minded lessons from cross-cultural negotiations into everyday negotiations? To deal well with another individual means understanding the way that person sees the world. At a minimum, negotiating requires not offending another person's sensibilities. Effective negotiating means being able to build a working relationship that encompasses respect for and understanding of another's beliefs. To treat all negotiations as cross-cultural is to question your own assumptions, enhance communication, and discover the cultural gaps that need to be filled in with understanding, empathy, and respect as you build an agreement.

STRATEGIES TO CROSS THE CULTURAL GAP

In Chapter 7, I discuss building a bridge to the other party as you make commitments. I now provide strategies to cross the cultural gap between negotiators.

Assume You Don't Know Everything

Test what you learn. When you travel to a foreign country, you are more likely to question your assumptions about how to appropriately interact with people than you would when you're home. You might become more sensitive to the impact of your words and behavior. You might ask more questions. This mindset can be useful for any negotiation. By taking a more honestly inquisitive and curious mindset, you are less likely to miscommunicate or misunderstand. Check your understanding, ask follow-up questions, dig for underlying rationales, and regularly summarize progress in your negotiation.

Acknowledge That Your Perceptions Are Limited

Share your perceptions *as perceptions*. In an explicitly cross-cultural situation, you are more likely to assume there is something you're missing, that you don't have all the information, or that there's a history you aren't aware of. Perhaps you will recognize that because your nationality is different, you just *see* things differently. Why not think more like this in your everyday negotiations?

In everyday negotiations, you are more likely to sense you are right and the other party is, well, not as right. Negotiation can succeed only when you and your negotiating partner learn how you each perceive a situation in a unique way.

Tell Your Story and Listen to Theirs

Keep in mind that individuals negotiate; cultures do not. Rather than assuming or projecting your understanding of someone else, share what makes you "you" and listen to the other person's story as well. Everything he says and does communicates his story. Ask questions to learn more. At the same time, help the other party by sharing your story, what is important to you, and how you have become the negotiator you are. Often this storytelling takes place away from the table in an informal setting. Don't underestimate the value of these opportunities.

Understand Intent, but Share Impact

When words or actions surprise you—especially if they run counter to your sensibilities—attempt to understand the intent or purpose of the person. Say something like, "I'm not sure what you're trying to achieve. It would help me if I could learn more about your goals here." Share the impact on you of a given statement to help the other person understand and to move the conversation forward.

Learn about the Other Party's "Culture"

It helps to understand the cultures—corporate, governmental, family, and so on—of the people you interact with. Knowing this can help prevent miscommunication and misunderstanding, and it can help smooth interactions. It can also demonstrate an effort to build rapport. Many negotiators extol the value of informal time spent together: "We get more done during lunch than we do during the formal meeting." At the same time, be careful with this knowledge. Having information about a person's culture can be misleading and even wrong when applied to a particular individual. Use this information to increase understanding, test assumptions, and increase empathy.

Monitor and Be Sensitive to Perceptions of Power and Respect

Individuals often perceive each other through the lens of power. Awareness of this can help break through the walls that perceptions of power can create. Distrust and suspicion often follow perceptions of power, so be sensitive of this dynamic in order to improve relationships.

If you're concerned that someone distrusts you because you are in a position of power, inclusiveness may reduce distrust. Say things like, "Before we approach this problem, I want to make sure I get everyone's input." Be more transparent and explicit about goals, agenda, and motives to help prevent misunderstanding and suspicion. Monitor whether the individual across the table feels respected. Showing respect will help you frame what you say and do in ways that build rapport.

Build Trust

Do things early on to build trust in your relationship. Give the other person the benefit of the doubt and initiate cooperation and goodwill—be willing to trust if they aren't yet. When a gap exists because you don't know each other, there may be no trust or perhaps there may even be mistrust. You cannot control how trusting the other person is, but you can control how trustworthy you are. Your trustworthy behavior can help build the bridge. Give your counterpart the benefit of the doubt to create a grace period for bridge-building. For example, if the behavior of a person you're starting to work with seems odd, rather than jumping to a negative conclusion you might inquire, "I'm interested in what you did here. Can you tell me more about it?" Your efforts to increase mutual trust will serve you well when you try to deal with the differences that, by definition, exist in a negotiation setting.

See Your Own Culture

Perhaps the best thing you can focus on to do all of the above is to look at your own background. This is not as easy as it sounds. Your own culture is often invisible to you but plainly visible to others. Dealing with someone different from you and truly understanding how she sees you may raise issues you may have never dealt with before. The greater your personal insight, the more likely it is that you will be able to see who you are to others.

When you spend time in another culture, you have the chance to see beyond generalizations and experience the intricacies of that culture. And it may help you see your own culture for the first time. Americans often remark that they never feel more American than when they live abroad, and at the same time they feel more sensitized to recognizing similarities between America and other cultures.

The take-home message in cross-cultural negotiating is to be honest, open, and sensitive. The more you truly engage the other party, the more you will see and understand your differences and commonalities, and the better able you will be to work together toward a constructive, mutually satisfying solution.

Act with a Clear Conscience

CHALLENGE

Ditko wins a collection of *Spiderman* comic books in a school fund-raiser. He is told that the comics have a value of $6,000. Ditko, who knows little about comic book values, does not research any further the actual value of the *Spiderman* comics and places an ad on the Internet to sell the comics. Kirby, a potential buyer responds. Ditko tells Kirby that he has another buyer who is offering to buy his collection for $6,500, which is false. Ditko also explains that he is willing to accept nothing less than $6,500 even though he would be willing to accept $5,500.

Kirby, who is a comic book expert, notices that one of the *Spiderman* comics contains a misprint, and there are three known copies. Kirby knows that the average sale price of the last three times a copy of this comic has been sold is $30,000. Kirby does not inform Ditko of this fact. Kirby says he can pay no more than $5,000, but actually is willing to pay $28,000. Eventually Ditko sells the entire collection to Kirby for $6,100.

DISCUSSION

Negotiations often happen in private, which makes unethical behavior, specifically lying, difficult to detect or monitor. Most cultures including the United States have standards that allow for bluffing and puffery in negotiations. For example, when Ditko says to Kirby, an avid collector, that he will accept nothing less than $6,500, even though he would be willing to agree to $5,500, while Kirby says he can only pay $5,000, but actually is willing to pay $28,000, most people would find that acceptable. Some negotiation experts will even go so far as saying that deception and subterfuge are intrinsic to negotiations. Whether you lie or use subterfuge or not, it is important to recognize that people you face may, and you need to be prepared.

Some might find Ditko, claiming that he had another buyer when he in fact did not, problematic. Others might not. When faced with an ethical dilemma, first ask yourself the question of whether you are comfortable with the tactic, and second, consider whether another less problematic approach is as effective or more effective. I would argue that Ditko would have been better off doing more research into the comic books' value and finding more buyers that would then have made his claim 100 percent true.

Whether Kirby should share the information that one piece of the collection is worth $30,000 strikes me as different. I do not think Kirby should be held responsible for Ditko's ignorance or lack of expertise and research. This is akin to a person finding a copy of the Declaration of Independence at a flea market.

ASK YOURSELF THE RIGHT QUESTIONS

When it comes to discussing ethics, the danger is to come off preachy. At the same time, if we do not consider the ethical aspects of a negotiation, you are not truly ready to deal with potentially difficult scenarios that will bubble up. My goal here as in other sections of the book is to turn the focus on you, the reader, and ask good questions to enable you to be fully prepared and to get the best results in terms of substantive outcome, relationships, and feeling morally comfortable with your own actions.

With respect to matters of disclosure, another important ethical issue involves how to deal with one's leverage. If there has been a hurricane in Florida and drinking water is at a premium, societal standards tell us that jacking up the price to what the market can afford is wrong. If the other party vastly underestimates the value of her asset, at what point does it become unconscionable to take advantage of that knowledge? A number of states require homeowners to disclose substantial problems in their homes when they are selling it. However, in most situations, it is still "buyer [or negotiator] beware."

The temptation to respond to unethical behavior with unethical behavior can be strong. What I would advocate is that under circumstances where you are tempted to misrepresent or omit important facts, consider other ways of achieving the outcome you are seeking without resorting to misrepresentation or omission. The methods in this book provide approaches that will work in response to unethical behavior. Let us say that Ditko notices Kirby spending a lot of time looking at the misprinted comic. Ditko asks whether there is anything special about that comic book. An effective negotiator would then continue down this line and ask more interest and criteria questions. If Ditko is skilled at ICON analysis, he either would have done research beforehand and found out about the high value of a misprinted version, or he would have taken a step back from the negotiation to do additional research. Ditko would have then negotiated with the necessary knowledge to not get taken advantage of.

The challenge that exists in negotiation ethics lies at the intersection of zealous advocacy for what you want and the resulting temptation to misrepresent in doing so. To effectively deal with the temptation means to reflect on both your internal sense of what's right and ethical codes and guidelines that exist.

The problem is that lying is often effective, and some forms of it are seen as acceptable within negotiation. It is important to acknowledge the broad temptation which leads to its frequent practice, so as not to be naïve as to what actually happens there. At the same time, one can make choices as to what industry one practices, as misrepresentation is more frequent in certain types of transactions and less frequent in others. You can then reflect on your individual approach, and just as importantly, your response to unethical behavior.

Another component to consider is whether the action you are considering might reduce the level of trust. Clearly this matters more in a balanced concern situation as opposed to a transactional one. However, even in a transactional situation, it can backfire if discovered either for that specific transaction or a future one. Separate your behavior from what the other side is doing and what it might do. Regardless, you may want to act in a trustworthy manner.

In working through your approach, you can examine your values and your beliefs. This may certainly involve complexities, contradictions, and subtleties. To be helpful, here are a few short, concise questions to ask yourself when a situation poses potential ethical dilemmas.

How Would Someone Important to You Evaluate the Behavior You Are Considering?

For example, if your parents, spouse, or children knew what you were doing, what would they think? The exercise of doing this provides a simple way to reflect on your own values. It also serves as a clear reminder of a source of your belief system. Even if you have a very different set of beliefs from, say, your parents, this process provides a way of stepping to the proverbial balcony and perceiving your situation from a different, yet familiar perspective. Reflect on how someone you respect immensely—a mentor from work, maybe even a former professor—might view what you're considering and determine whether they might handle such a situation similarly or differently. Even go to a historical or current figure whom you consider a role model and imagine how this person would think and act. How would Eleanor Roosevelt, Mahatma Gandhi, or Abraham Lincoln have viewed and handled the situation?

What Would You Feel If What You Did Appeared on the Internet or in a Newspaper?

This exercise provides a similar filter, albeit from a public perspective. Negotiation often happens behind closed doors, and we often act in ways in private that we would not if we were observed or if our behavior was known by others. While it is true that some people regret being caught rather than the behavior itself, pondering what it means to be caught is helpful for everyone to seriously consider. Actually visualizing a story in a newspaper, a blog, or television news report brings home the possible shame or embarrassment that you could experience.

What Does the Golden Rule Tell You?

You have likely heard the Golden Rule: "Do unto others as you would have them do unto you." So if someone else did whatever tactic you are considering, would you be okay with that? Many people use this rule as a standard for their actions. However, it is easy to forget in the heat of negotiation, so it is useful to apply this fundamental approach. Of course, just because you use this standard doesn't mean the other party will. Recognize that in many transactional and high-stakes negotiations, the norm may be deception, and parties within that world accept that. Even in those situations it is still your choice of how you act. Whatever your choice, be prepared for the other side not using the Golden Rule.

What Advice Would You Give Others?

Ethical quandaries can be paralyzing. By imagining you are giving advice to someone else in the same situation, you can find your own voice. If it was your best friend or a coworker facing the choice, what would you tell that person? Also, consider what questions you would ask that person in order to delve into the complexities and subtleties of the dilemma. Your values and sense of ethics can then bubble to the surface. You likely have the answer within you, but the conflicting desires and stress are blocking you.

If you have an ethical dilemma in your current situation, answer the following questions:

- How would someone important to you evaluate the behavior you are considering?
- How would you feel if what you did was reported on the Internet or in a newspaper?
- What does the Golden Rule tell you?
- What advice would you give others?

PART FOUR

APPENDIX

This section contains the following resources:

- ICON and 4D Summary
- 4D Key Points Summary
- Worksheets
- Glossary
- References
- About Accordence
- About the Author

Worksheets are reprinted in this section so you can use them again for different negotiations. We have also included summary descriptions of the ICON model and the 4D process, a glossary, references, and more information about Accordence and the author.

Prepare! Prepare! Prepare!

The best way to approach a competition, debate, performance, negotiation, or any big event is to prepare thoroughly, and then just let go. Don't get caught up in trying to remember a thousand details. Too much thinking can get in the way. The ICON and 4D worksheets you filled out in this guide are geared toward organizing the things you *already* know (or should know) about your negotiation. If you have truly done your preparation, then it's important to relax and rely on your experience, knowledge, and expertise.

My advice is to fill out some sort of ICON planner—like the ones you used in this book or like the QuickPrep Negotiation Planner I'll show you in this section—at the beginning of the negotiation cycle. As you learn more, you can add to it. For small negotiations, you can fill out a planner in 10 minutes. You may need to fill out only the ICON portions and never have to get into 4D. However, where strategy is important—especially for more complex negotiations or a more challenging negotiation dynamic— it may be critical to do your 4D homework too. Before each meeting, review the relevant portions of your planner. For the 4D information, look carefully each time at the design step, making sure that you have a solid foundation for your negotiation.

I'm not trying to change you as a person. I would like to make you a better negotiator, though. Preparation is the key. The more relaxed and comfortable you are in a negotiation, the more you will be able to listen, adjust to shifting circumstances and tactics, and expand the pie.

THE QUICKPREP NEGOTIATION PLANNER

Accordence uses a QuickPrep Negotiation Planner to help organize lists of Interests, Options, Criteria, and No-Agreement Alternatives. While any organizational setup is helpful, Accordence has thoroughly road-tested this one and found that it works quite well.

A blank planner is shown on the opposite page. Turn the page and look at this same form filled out with information you encountered for a case featured earlier in this guide—the one involving Brian, Christina, and the piano in the apartment complex. Remember that planners like this are generally filled out by just one side—in this case, Brian—so the ICON and 4D elements for the other party are all estimated. As with any negotiation, the estimations and assumptions made during preparation must be tested and validated (or invalidated) while conducting the negotiation itself.

To prepare for challenging negotiations, I also recommend role-playing with a friend or colleague—not to script your negotiation, but to get ready for different scenarios. It's like going through a dress rehearsal or running a scrimmage. You might be surprised at how valuable it can be to preview the dialogue as it might play out.

My final advice boils down to prepare, then prepare some more, and finally, prepare again. If this is the only thing you remember from this guide 10 years from now, then you will have retained the key lesson I want to impart. Use the ICON and 4D methods and planners to help you prepare. Thorough preparation is the most effective way to improve your skills and outcomes.

What do I recommend you do after preparing? Relax! Just let the information flow out naturally, and you'll be more instinctive and smooth. Internalize the lessons from your preparation, and from the ICON and 4D lessons taught in this guide, and you will have a road map for creating more value—for expanding the pie—in all of your negotiations, from the home to the boardroom and beyond!

Good luck!

QuickPrep Negotiation Planner

Date:		
Negotiator:		
Situation:		
GOALS	**AGENDA**	**DIALOGUE**
Substance:		Core Message:
Relationship:		

INTERESTS (subjective)			
Ours			Theirs

OPTIONS (on the table) (circle BPA)			**CRITERIA** (objective)

NO-AGREEMENT ALTERNATIVES (away from the table) (circle BATNA)			
Ours			Theirs

ICON and 4D Summary

ICON SUMMARY

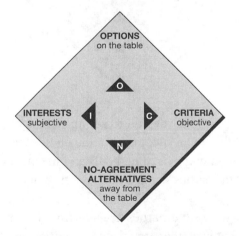

Interests are the motivators, needs, drivers, concerns, and fears of the parties. They are the foundation for the entire negotiation.

Criteria are objective benchmarks, precedents, and standards of legitimacy that help you filter and judge the best options. Savvy negotiators come to the table with a good understanding of the relevant benchmarks, even before anything is agreed to.

ssible solutions that the parties might agree to for sat-
r shared, differing, and conflicting interests.

t **Alternatives** are what the parties will do if they walk
away from the negotiation without coming to any agreement.

4D SUMMARY

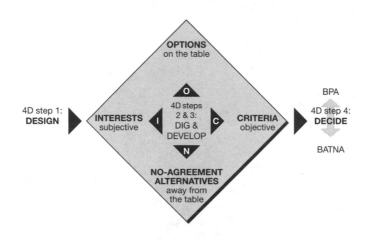

Design is what the parties do to set up the negotiation for success.
Your ability to be successful at the end depends on what you do
in the beginning by setting goals and having a clear plan.

Dig is what the parties say and do in order to understand each other's
needs.

Develop is where the parties create win-win options to solve the
problem at hand that are fair to the parties involved.

Decide is where the parties come to closure by either committing to
a final agreement or walking away.

4D Key Points Summary

Keep these key points in mind as you go through the 4D process of your negotiation. Each of these points was mentioned in the 4D Key Point boxes in Part Two:

- Preparing for your negotiation will make all the difference.
- Until you create value, any price is too high.
- Be assertive on both the substance and the relationship.
- When team negotiating, provide specific roles to individuals.
- When emotions run high, stop focusing on the problem and start focusing on the people.
- Negotiating is an interactive activity, so you won't always do everything in a strict order.
- Discussing no-agreement alternatives is a critical tool of win-win negotiating.
- Respond to position or demand statements with interest questions.
- You can use an expand-the-pie approach regardless of what the other side does.

- Effective negotiators don't just listen to words, they listen for what the other side really cares about.
- Be assertive with interests, flexible with options.
- Walk directly to the BATNA instead of being defensive.
- Strive for a better deal for all parties as you get closer to final agreement.
- When you get stuck, go back to underlying interests. Discipline, persistence, and patience will pay off.
- Remember to summarize your agreements.

Use the worksheet below to list other key points you found useful in this guide:

Other Key Points

_____

_____

_____

_____

_____

_____

_____

_____

_____

_____

_____

_____

_____

_____

Worksheets

The following worksheets are the ones you may have filled out earlier in this guide. Use these as replacement worksheets for the negotiation you were working on, or fill them out for new negotiations.

1. With whom are you negotiating? (person, position, experience, organization)

_____

_____

_____

2. List at least three key pieces of background information on this negotiation.

_____

_____

_____

3. Why is this negotiation a challenging one for you?

_____

_____

_____

_____

Interests	Type	Priority
Yours		
Theirs		
Other Stakeholders		

Type	Priority
S=shared	H=high
D=differing	M=medium
C=conflicting	L=low

Options	MPA	BPA

Check options that serve as part of BPA and/or MPA.

Criteria	Persuasive?

Check criteria that may be persuasive to the other party.

No-Agreement Alternatives	BATNA
Yours	
Theirs	

Check your BATNA and theirs.

Design Checklist

Set Goals

    a)   Substance:

    b)   Relationship:

Construct an Agenda

    a)   Agenda:

    b)   Ground rules:

    c)   Roles:

Deliver a Core Message

    a)   Core message:

Digging for Interests

Their Position_____

_____

_____

_____

_____

Their Possible Interests _____

_____

_____

_____

_____

_____

_____

Your Interests Questions _____

_____

_____

_____

_____

_____

_____

Developing Options

Criteria Questions to Ask _____

_____

_____

_____

_____

_____

_____

_____

_____

_____

Criteria Statements _____

_____

_____

_____

_____

_____

_____

_____

_____

Dig and Develop Checklist

1. Discover interests

a) What questions will probe for the other party's interests?

b) What interests do you want to share? What interests do you *not* want to disclose?

2. Brainstorm options

a) What options might you try to draw out?

(*continued on next page*)

Dig and Develop Checklist

b) What options do you want to put on the table? What options do you *not* want on the table?

3. Narrow through criteria

a) What questions might you ask to find helpful criteria?

b) What criteria statements will you provide? What criteria will you *not* provide?

4. Ready no-agreement alternatives

a) Will you disclose your BATNA?

b) If you do disclose, how will you do it?

c) Will you ask about the other party's BATNA, and if so, how?

INFORMATION EXCHANGE WORKSHEET

For an upcoming negotiation, fill out the following:

Get: (questions to ask)

Give: (information to disclose)

Guard: (information to protect)

Closure Strategies

Closure Strategy_____

_____

_____

_____

Sample Dialogue _____

_____

_____

_____

_____

_____

Decide Checklist

1. Aim for the Best Possible Agreement (BPA)

a) What is the Best Possible Agreement?

b) What is your Minimum Possible Agreement?

2. Make tentative agreements

a) What tentative agreements might you offer or accept in this meeting?

3. Take the next steps

a) What are the next steps that will get you closer to an agreement on substance?

4. Get both parties on the same side

a) What steps will you take to ensure that you and the other party are on the same side?

Glossary

Agenda: The process you will use for this meeting or for the negotiation as a whole to get to the substance and relationship goals you have determined.

Anchoring: The phenomenon by which exposure to even arbitrary or biased numbers changes a negotiator's assessment of what an agreement should be.

BATNA (Best Alternative to a Negotiated Agreement): The no-agreement alternative that best meets a single party's interests. BATNA is a form of self-help—an alternative that can be accomplished without agreement from the other party.

Best Possible Agreement: The package of options that best meets the interests of all parties.

Bottom Line: Also called reservation point or minimum possible agreement. It is the least a party is willing to agree to rather than walk away with no agreement.

Concession: Value yielded or committed by one party to the other.

Concessional Bargaining: See *Win-Lose Negotiating*.

Conflicting Interests: Parties' needs that are in direct tension with one another.

Core Message: The theme a negotiator will stick to throughout the negotiation. This theme often seeks to integrate both substance and relationship.

Creating Value: See *Expanding the Pie*.

Criteria: Precedents, benchmarks, and standards. These serve as objective means to filter or narrow options.

Differing Interests: Parties desire things that are not the same but that are not at odds.

Dividing the Pie: Distributing value in a negotiation—the who-gets-what aspect.

Expanding the Pie: If the total value in a negotiation is represented by a pie, then an expansion of the pie occurs when the total value is increased. This can happen because a new option is introduced or an interest is met in a better way than before. The expanded value can take the form of money, time, effort, respect, and more.

4D: The 4D approach—Design, Dig, Develop, and Decide—is a start-to-finish preparation, analysis, and decision-making strategy for a negotiation. Use this approach to put ICON into play.

ICON: Interests, Criteria, Options, and No-Agreement Alternatives. These four elements are the building blocks and substance of a negotiation. Start by discovering interests, then develop options, filter these through criteria, and assess your no-agreement alternatives.

Interests: The subjective needs, goals, drivers, concerns, and fears of the parties. Interests are different from positions, which are the demands of a party, or a fixation on one option.

Issues: Specific items, points, questions, or categories that are to be discussed and decided in a negotiation.

Leverage: The power or ability to act or to influence people or decisions.

Minimum Possible Agreement: Also called the bottom line or reservation value. The least satisfactory package of options a party can agree to that will meet his or her interests.

Negotiation: A discussion to reach agreement. Involves parties attempting to persuade or influence each other.

Next Steps: Actions both parties make together, or either party makes unilaterally, to move the negotiation closer to agreement.

No-Agreement Alternatives: The walkaway possibilities that each party has if no agreement is reached. This is different from an option, which all parties must agree to. A BATNA is the best no-agreement alternative a party may have.

Opening Line: Your first words to initiate the key discussion in a negotiation or meeting.

Options: Possible solutions to satisfy interests. These are the possibilities that parties agree or say yes to. These are distinguished from no-agreement alternatives, which one party will arrive at without the agreement of the other party.

Position: A specific demand focused on one option or package of options.

Positional: The approach to a negotiation of making specific demands.

Relationship Goal: What you would like the individual working relationship between the parties to be as a result of a negotiation or specific meeting.

Relationship Value: The quality of the relationship developed between parties in a negotiation.

Shared Interests: Needs that parties have in common.

Substance Goal: What you would like to see accomplished as a result of a negotiation or specific meeting.

Substance Value: The quality of the outcome of a negotiation—its terms, solutions, and so on.

Tentative Agreement: An option agreed to and set aside temporarily to move the decision-making process forward. In the end, the ability to come to final agreement is contingent upon the whole being acceptable.

Test of Reciprocity: The test of whether one party is willing to do the equivalent of what the other party is asked to do.

Win-Lose Negotiating: Also called distributive or concessional bargaining. This is an approach to negotiating wherein the parties involved attempt to gain at the expense of the other.

Win-Win Negotiating: Also called interest-based or joint-gain negotiating. This is an approach to negotiating wherein the parties involved strive to achieve an agreement that is highly satisfactory to everyone.

References

Arrow, Kenneth, Robert Mnookin, Lee Ross, Amos Tversky, and Robert Wilson. 1995. *Barriers to Conflict Resolution.* New York: Norton.

Axelrod, Robert M. 1994. *The Evolution of Cooperation.* New York: Basic Books.

Bazerman, Max H., and Margaret Ann Neale. 1992. *Negotiating Rationally.* New York: Free Press.

Brams, Steven, and Alan D. Taylor. 2000. *The Win-Win Solution: Guaranteeing Fair Shares to Everybody.* New York: Norton.

Breslin, J. William, and Jeffrey Z. Rubin, eds. 1991. *Negotiation Theory and Practice.* Cambridge, MA: Program on Negotiation Books.

Cialdini, Robert B. 2006. *Influence: The Psychology of Persuasion.* New York: Collins Business Essentials.

Dixit, Avinash K., and Barry Nalebuff. 1991. *Thinking Strategically: The Competitive Edge in Business, Politics, and Everyday Life.* New York: Norton.

Doyle, Michael, and David Straus. 1976. *How to Make Meetings Work: The New Interaction Method.* New York: Jove Books.

Fisher, Roger, and Scott Brown. 1988. *Getting Together: Building Relationships as We Negotiate.* Boston: Houghton Mifflin. (Paperback edition published by Penguin Books, New York, 1988.)

Fisher, Roger, and Danny Ertel. 1995. *Getting Ready to Negotiate: The Getting to Yes Workbook.* New York: Penguin Books.

Fisher, Roger, Elizabeth Kopelman, and Andrea Kupfer Schneider. 1994. *Beyond Machiavelli: Coping with Conflict.* Cambridge, MA: Harvard University Press.

Fisher, Roger, and Alan Sharp. 1998. *Getting It Done: How to Lead When You Are Not in Charge.* New York: HarperCollins.

Fisher, Roger, and William L. Ury. 1978. *International Mediation: A Working Guide—Ideas for the Practitioners.* Cambridge, MA: Harvard Negotiation Project.

Fisher, Roger, William L. Ury, and Bruce Patton. 1991. *Getting to Yes: Negotiating Agreement without Giving In.* 2d ed. New York: Penguin Books.

Freshman, Clark, and Chris Guthrie. 2009. "Managing the Goal-Setting Paradox: How to Get Better Results from High Goals and Be Happy," *Negotiation Journal*, vol. 25, p. 217.

Gilligan, Carol. 1993. *In a Different Voice: Psychological Theory and Women's Development.* Cambridge, MA: Harvard University Press.

Harvard Business Review on Negotiation and Conflict Resolution. 2000. Cambridge, MA: Harvard Business School Press.

Hofstede, Geert. 1997. *Cultures and Organizations: Software of the Mind.* New York: McGraw-Hill.

Kahneman, Daniel, and Amos Tversky. 1979. "Prospect Theory: An Analysis of Decision under Risk," *Econometrica,* vol. 47, p. 2.

Kilmann, Ralph H., and Kenneth W. Thomas. "Developing a Forced-Choice Measure of Conflict-Handling Behavior: The 'MODE' Instrument," *Educational and Psychological Measurement,* vol. 37, pp. 309–325.

Korobkin, Russell. 2009. *Negotiation: Theory and Strategy.* New York. Aspen Law and Business.

Latz, Martin E. 2004. *Gain the Edge! Negotiating to Get What You Want.* New York: St. Martin's Press.

Lax, David A., and James K. Sebenius. 1986. *The Manager as Negotiator: Bargaining for Cooperation and Competitive Gain.* New York: Free Press.

Lord, Charles G., Lee Ross, and Mark R. Lepper. 1979. "Biased Assimilation and Attitude Polarization: The Effects of Prior Theories on Subsequently Considered Evidence," *Journal of Personality and Social Psychology,* vol. 37, p. 11.

Machiavelli, Niccolo. 1513. *The Prince.* Mark Musa trans. 1964. New York: St. Martin's Press.

Mcnkcl-Mcadow, Carrie, Lela Love, and Andrea Schneider. 2006. *Negotiation: Processes for Problem Solving.* New York: Aspen Publishing.

Mnookin, Robert H., Scott R. Peppet, and Andrew S. Tulumello. 2000. *Beyond Winning: Negotiating to Create Value in Deals and Disputes.* Cambridge, MA: Harvard University Press.

Nelken, Melissa. 2005. "The Myth of the Gladiator and Law Students' Negotiation Styles," *Cardozo Journal of Conflict Resolution*, vol. 7, p. 1.

Nelken, Melissa. 2007. *Negotiation Theory and Practice.* Newark, NJ: LexisNexis.

Northcraft, Gregory B., and Margaret A. Neale. 1987. "Experts, Amateurs, and Real Estate: An Anchoring-and-Adjustment Perspective on Property Pricing Decisions," *Organizational Behavior and Human Decision Processes,* vol. 39, p. 1.

Pedersen, Paul B., and Fred E. Jandt, eds. 1996. *Constructive Conflict Management: Asia Pacific Cases.* Thousand Oaks, CA: Sage Publications.

Raiffa, Howard. 1982. *The Art and Science of Negotiation.* Cambridge, MA: Harvard University Press.

Ross, Lee. 1995. "Reactive Devaluation in Negotiation and Conflict Resolution," in *Barriers to Conflict Resolution,* Kenneth J. Arrow et al., eds. New York: Norton.

Rubin, Jeffrey Z., Dean G. Pruitt, and Sung Hee Kim. 1994. *Social Conflict: Escalation, Stalemate, and Settlement.* 2d ed. New York: McGraw-Hill.

Salem, Paul. 1993. "A Critique of Western Conflict Resolution from a Non-Western Perspective," *Negotiation Journal,* October, vol. 9, p. 3.

Schelling, Thomas C. 1960. *The Strategy of Conflict.* Cambridge, MA: Harvard University Press.

Schneider, Andrea Kupfer, and Michael Moffitt. 2008. *Dispute Resolution: Examples and Explanations.* New York: Aspen.

Shell, G. Richard. 2006. *Bargaining for Advantage: Negotiation Strategies for Reasonable People.* 2d ed. New York: Penguin Books.

Stone, Douglas, Bruce Patton, and Sheila Heen. 1999. *Difficult Conversations: How to Discuss What Matters Most.* New York: Penguin Books.

Tannen, Deborah. 1990. *You Just Don't Understand: Women and Men in Conversation.* New York: Ballantine Books.

Thomas, Kenneth W., and Ralph H. Kilmann. 2009. Thomas-Kilmann Conflict Mode Instrument. Available at www.kilmann.com/conflict.html.

Thompson, Leigh, and Dennis Hrebec. 1996. "Lose-Lose Agreements in Interdependent Decision Making," *Psychological Bulletin*, vol. 120, pp. 396–409.

Ury, William L. 1991. *Getting Past No: Negotiating with Difficult People.* New York: Bantam Books.

Walton, Richard E., and Robert B. McKersie. 1991. *A Behavioral Theory of Labor Negotiations: An Analysis of a Social Interaction System.* 2d ed. Ithaca, NY: ILR Press.

Wanis-St. John, Anthony. 1996. "Managers as Negotiators: The Power and Gender Mix," *Negotiation Journal*, vol. 12, p. 4.

Watkins, Michael, and Samuel Passow. 1996. "Analyzing Linked Systems of Negotiations," *Negotiation Journal,* vol. 12, p. 4.

Weiss, Stephen E. 1994. "Negotiating with "Romans—Part 1," *Sloan Management Review,* winter, vol. 35, p, 2.

Weiss, Stephen E. 1994. "Negotiating with "Romans—Part 2," *Sloan Management Review*, spring, vol. 35, p. 3.

Wilson, Marie G., Gregory B. Northcraft, and Margaret A. Neale. 1989. "Information Competition and Vividness Effects in On-line Judgements," *Organizational Behavior and Human Decision Processes,* vol. 44, p. 1.

About Accordence

I hope you have found this guide useful for improving your negotiation skills. This guide is just a primer for some situations, however. Complex or high-stakes negotiations often require the intervention of a third party. Through facilitation, mediation, consulting, and customized training, Accordence helps prepare for and conduct effective negotiations and build good working relationships among stakeholders.

Accordence clients include Acxiom, American Century, American Express, Amgen, BP, Cadence Design, Cap Gemini Ernst & Young, Charles Schwab, DuPont, Eastman Chemical, Eli Lilly, Elsevier, Hewlett-Packard, Kodak, Lawrence Livermore Labs, Microsoft Business Solutions, Nova Nordisk, the Red Cross, Tripwire, and Xerox.

For more information, contact us at:
Accordence
533 Airport Boulevard, Suite 400
Burlingame, CA 94010
(650) 200-3077
inquiry@accordence.com
www.accordence.com

About the Author

Grande Lum is clinical professor of law and director of the Center for Negotiation and Dispute Resolution at the University of California Hastings College of the Law. He is serving as director of the Small Business Administration's HUBZone program for the Obama administration. Lum is also the founder and former managing director of Accordence, a negotiation consulting and training firm.

Lum has mediated labor-management disputes, advised companies on partnering and alliances, and provided negotiation training and facilitation services. He has produced a negotiation video and written a number of articles on negotiations and collaborative processes, been a regular contributor to Huffington Post and was formerly a partner at Conflict Management Inc., a consulting firm cofounded by *Getting to Yes* coauthor and Harvard law professor Roger Fisher. Lum is also cofounder and former principal of ThoughtBridge. He is a graduate of the University of California, Berkeley, and Harvard Law School.

Index

Notes

Notes

Notes

Notes

Notes

Notes

Notes

Notes

Notes

Notes